when
HOPE
ends
life begins

FREYA BARKER

To Michelle,
Happy Reading!

xox *[signature]*

ISBN: 9781988733456
Cover Design: **Freya Barker**
Editing: **Karen Hrdlicka**
Proofing: **Joanne Thompson**

WHEN HOPE ENDS

It's the best day of his life—the worst of hers.

She left her soul behind in the dead silence of a hospital room.
He is bright with hope after being so close to losing faith.

One moment in time leaves their paths unavoidably entwined.
An invisible connection held by one heart beating between them.

Prologue

Mika

"I'M SORRY, Mr. Ainsworth, but on this I have to agree with Ms. Spencer."

The relief I feel at Judge Winslow's words, walking out of the courtroom, is short-lived. The reality hits me in the face the moment I step into Kenny G's holiday classics streaming into the otherwise empty elevator cab. My knees buckle and I end up on my ass, sitting on the floor with my back against the side.

The frenzied battle waged in and out of the courtroom, these past five days, suddenly seems insignificant in the face of what's ahead. Today, in fact. The judge ended up giving Emmett and his family until four this afternoon to say their goodbyes, and after that it will all be up to me.

The heaviest of responsibilities my knees clearly can't hold up under.

The moment the door hisses open, I'm blinded by flashing lights.

1

Stupid. I'd all but forgotten they were here.

I scramble to my feet, an endeavor made more difficult with microphones and recording devices shoved in my face, and block out the questions that come at me from all directions. Hard to believe I was part of the pack not that long ago.

I should've let Sam come. When I talked to her briefly this morning and she mentioned Demi—her youngest—had been sick all night, I insisted she stay home and look after her. I regret it now. Sam would've plowed her way through the small crowd of my peers and hustled me out of there.

I will myself not to show emotion, a copy of the judge's order being crumpled in my hand from the effort. I fight the panic crawling up my throat as they hold the elevator doors open, but block me inside. My eyes aim over their heads to look for help.

It comes in the form of a gray, potbellied security guard who comes to my rescue. He forces himself through the throng and grabs me by the arm. I follow behind him like a frightened child, as he drags me into a small room beside the security checkpoint at the door.

"Breathe," my Good Samaritan orders. "Where the hell is your lawyer?"

"Another case," I manage, trying to control my breathing.

"Do you have a car or should I call someone to pick you up?"

"Just a taxi, please."

I'd left my car at the hospital. Driving in Boston is a nightmare on the best of days. I had no desire to get stuck finding a parking spot, so I opted to cab it.

Ten minutes later, the same kind guard leads me down the courthouse steps and into the cab waiting below.

"Tufts, please."

"Which entrance?" the driver asks.

"Emergency," I quickly say, hoping to avoid the press likely to be hounding the main entrance, as they have the past few days, since Emmett made our battle a very public one.

My job, not so long ago my passion, has turned on me these past weeks. Even after being out of the spotlight the past nine months, unfortunately I'm apparently still newsworthy. Of course, Emmett and his parents are mostly to blame for that, probably thinking I would cave under public pressure.

I haven't. Not when the only redeeming outcome in this nightmare was dependent on my strength.

The emergency entrance to the otherwise busy hospital is blissfully quiet, and I send up a brief thank you to whatever power is up there. For one who's not particularly religious, I've sure sent up my share of prayers these past nine months and even more so the past week. Pretty sure no one is listening, but even knowing intellectually there's no avoiding what is coming, I'm not willing to leave any stone unturned.

On the third floor, I force myself to grab a coffee and a sandwich, knowing I'll need to keep up my strength. Besides, Emmett and his parents are probably with him already. They left the courthouse while I was waiting for a copy of the order.

They have another hour before it's my turn, time I need to set the wheels in motion. Lives may depend on it.

———

"ARE YOU READY?"

Swallowing hard, I'm only able to nod.

It's probably been close to an hour since Emmett was escorted out by security. His parents were already gone, but he'd lingered, waiting for me to arrive. He didn't hesitate

3

making an ugly scene, flinging accusations I rationally know were without foundation in the truth, but he cut me nonetheless.

Deep.

His hurtful words teased the exposed nerve of guilt I couldn't help but feel, and I needed some time to reflect. Staff kept a respectful distance for a while, but with the clock ticking, I couldn't fault them for prodding me along.

The sudden silence in the room is deafening as I'm given a few moments alone with him. I stroke my fingers over his impassive face. It used to be the only thing that would soothe him, make him fall asleep.

I lean over the bed and kiss his face.

"Sleep tight, my love."

Then I walk out of the room, leaving my world behind.

Jude

"WHAT?"

I surge up from my chair and my heart stops in my throat at Cassie's words.

"They may have a heart," she repeats.

My body drops back down as I process what she's saying. "For Kelty? Oh my God."

"I know." Her voice is soft and I can hear her tears.

"I'm taking her right now. They want her in as soon as possible, so they can start prepping, but it'll probably be hours yet. How long will you be?"

I look around my messy office, and for once I wish I'd

picked Boston instead of Cape Cod to open my restaurant. "An hour," I answer, much too optimistically.

"Jude, please. You don't do anyone favors if you get pulled over, hurt, or—God forbid—killed because you're speeding. Maybe you should ask Steve to drive you."

Steve is one of the reasons I ended up in Orleans. I went to college with the guy and being a real estate agent on the Cape, when he got wind I was looking for a location, he started sending me prospective listings. I fell in love with a cove-side property just north of town right away and signed the papers just days after seeing it.

That was thirteen years ago and I've never regretted it until today.

"Mandy!" I call out as I grab my coat. It's fucking cold out, with a stiff wind blowing in off the water. Snow is expected after this weekend, but I suspect I'll be holed up in Boston.

I hope I'll still be in Boston.

"Yeah, Boss?"

Amanda Ross is my restaurant manager. She's a local who was the first to respond to my ad looking for staff thirteen years ago. Then a new high school graduate without a lot of prospects on the Cape. What she didn't have in formal education, she made up for over the years, learning on the job and in a few courses I paid for her to follow. Now thirty-one, Mandy is married to a local commercial fisherman—a great guy who happens to supply the restaurant with fresh catch—and she runs the day-to-day of Cove Side Cooker. On top of that, she's become a friend.

"I'm off to Tufts."

Her eyes go wide. "Kelty?"

"She's good. It's…" Suddenly my emotions get the better

5

of me and I struggle to get my next words out. "They may have a heart for her."

The next instant, my manager throws herself in my arms and drenches me with her tears, chanting, "Ohmigod, ohmigod…"

"Mandy, honey. I gotta go." My own eyes wet, I pry her away from me and kiss her forehead. "I gotta know you've got this place."

"Right." She wipes her sleeve over her wet face, fighting for composure as she starts shoving me out of the restaurant. "I've got it, Boss. Best get going. I'll let everyone know."

That gives me pause and I stop in my tracks.

"Maybe hold off on that? Until we know a bit more, okay?" I quickly add when her face shows immediate concern.

Maybe I'm being overly cautious, but if I've learned anything this past year, it's that nothing is guaranteed. Especially not good news.

"Of course," she immediately responds. "Keep me in the loop, though. I'll be praying for you all."

I'm one of those non-practicing Catholics, who still believes in the power of prayer. Nothing wrong with sending that positive energy out into the universe.

"Appreciated."

I give her a nervous smile and dart out to my Traverse in the parking lot.

"DADDY!"

My heart gives a jolt, seeing my nine-year-old, blue-eyed, blonde-haired princess back in a hospital bed. The only difference is, this time her smile is wide compared to the last time I walked into Tufts, finding a sickly girl hooked up to too many machines.

Since being diagnosed with acute cardiomyopathy, she's had a VAD—a ventricular assist device—surgically placed to give her failing heart a break. The last seven months, waiting on a viable heart, has been a lot better for her than the couple of months prior to that.

"Hey, Pooh." I close the distance to the bed and inhale her scent as I bend down, and she wraps her little arms around my neck.

"I'm getting my new heart today."

I love the sound of her girly, Tinker Bell voice and smile down on her. "So I hear."

My eyes immediately dart up to Cassie, who has her arms wrapped around her husband, Mark, both showing the overwhelming emotions I feel in my chest. Hope, apprehension, relief, and stark fear for what might lie ahead.

I kiss Kelty's curls before I get up from the bed and walk over to her mom.

Cassie lets go of Mark and she hugs me back as hard as I'm hugging her. Mark does the same when I turn to him.

We've been lucky.

Cassie and I never intended to have a child together. Ours was an occasional, convenient, and purely physical connection, but a pregnancy was the result of our friends-with-benefits arrangement. We weren't destined for anything more, and we both knew it. Agreeing to focus on co-parenting our child, and remain the friends we were—without the benefits part—was the best decision.

It was a year after Kelty was born Cassie met Mark, and although I'd been hesitant at first sharing my daughter with him, he proved to be a good man, a good stepfather to my daughter. The fact Kelty has three parents firmly in her corner has proven to be invaluable. Especially since early March of this year.

That's when Kelty first became sick.

"So it's official?" I ask, after everyone sits down. I'm perched on the side of our daughter's bed.

"Yes," Mark states firmly when Cassie only manages to nod.

I blow out an audible breath, hope and fear now dominating anything else I might feel.

We distract ourselves with inane chatter about the weather, sports, our respective jobs, interspersed with visits from the lab, an administrator with paperwork to sign, the anesthesiologist, and an OR nurse prepping Kelty. Finally the surgeon makes an appearance, reminding us he's done this surgery for many years to reassure us.

Not that it does, since this is and hopefully will be our first and only time, no matter how many of these transplant surgeries he's done over the years.

Still, when my princess is taken to the OR, and a nurse suggests we wait in the small surgical waiting room, I feel more hopeful than fearful.

"None of us have eaten. Why don't I go grab us something?" I offer, needing to do something. I've never been a particularly restful or patient person, I do better being active in some way.

"I don't think I could eat," Cassie voices.

"Something," I urge. "Even just some fruit or a yogurt. We'll likely be up all night, watching over her. You don't do her any favors if you collapse."

Throwing her own words back at her earns me an irritated glare. "Fine," she bites off.

"You stay," Mark suggests, getting up. "I'll grab us some sandwiches."

"It's okay. I need something to do," I assure him, resolutely walking out of the waiting room.

Straight into the path of a distraught-looking woman.

She looks vaguely familiar, although it's difficult to tell with her messy blonde tresses covering half of her face. Her business-like attire doesn't match the state of her face and hair.

"I'm sorry," she mumbles, pressing a hand to her mouth to stifle the sob that is visibly wracking her body.

Not sure why, but my hands immediately go to her shoulders to steady her. Her eyes shoot up and I see sheer torment in her pale gray, swollen eyes.

"Is there something I can do? Someone I can call, maybe?" I offer, my chest constricting in the face of her pain.

She abruptly shakes her head and turns away from my hold, and I just barely hear her response, before she hurries down the corridor.

"There's no one now."

Chapter One

Mika

"I DON'T UNDERSTAND why you need to do this?"

It's not the first time Sam has asked me this question, so I brush the hair out of my face and take in a deep breath before I try to explain again.

"Because I need a fresh start, Sam. It's been five months, and still two weeks ago I was blindsided by some gossip rag article that had pictures showing me visiting Jamie, and even one of me walking out of my therapist's office. It's ridiculous. Anywhere I look, every place I go; I'm reminded. How am I supposed to heal when every day rubs the wound raw, keeping it oozing?"

"But you don't know anyone there," she says, her face over the stack of boxes in my kitchen crumpling.

"Don't get me started," I warn her, but the next moment I'm engulfed in her embrace.

I love this woman. She's been my touchstone all our lives but literally became the rock I hung onto for dear life in the past year and change. Especially since right before Christmas, when Jamie died.

"Besides," I tell her, setting her back gently with my hands on her shoulders. "Not knowing anyone is kinda the point, Sam. I need to breathe instead of constantly gasping for the air that keeps getting knocked out of me."

"But who's going to be there if…well, if…"

I know what she's struggling with to say out loud. I was free-falling for a while after we buried Jamie, tumbling down a dark hole. With everything that gave me purpose gone, life just became…unbearable. It was Sam who found me and had to call an ambulance.

That was toward the end of January. I'd been so shocked at the stark pain in Sam's face when I woke up in the hospital. I'd been so lost in my dark vortex of grief; I lost the ability to see anything else. All I wanted was to numb the pain, but I ended up causing hers.

She felt betrayed—by me. That realization prompted me to agree to the six weeks of inpatient treatment I was offered. It gave me some parameters—and structure—things I needed until I could find my balance again.

It's disorienting when you no longer have responsibilities to carry or a schedule to keep. When the framework of your life is suddenly gone, and you no longer have any idea what to hold onto, or which direction to go.

"Honey," I whisper, lifting a hand to her cheek. "I'll be an hour and a half away. I'm keeping up with the weekly appointments at the clinic for now and will come to see you every time I'm in town. I'm not disappearing from the face of the earth." I dip my head to peek under her eyelashes. "I'm doing it to get out of this spiral that seems to want to pull me down. Don't you see? I'm not leaving you, I'm trying to find me."

"Mika, are you sure you…" Jason's voice trails off when he sees his wife in my arms and looks at me stunned. "What did I miss?"

"Mika's leaving, you big oaf," Sam snaps, swinging around on her husband, who already has his hands up defensively.

"Yeah, I got that part, since I've been hauling her furniture over to that storage place in Quincy all weekend."

"Exactly!" Sam throws her arms in the air and promptly starts crying again. Poor Jason looks at me with his eyes bugging, but luckily has the sense to pull her into a hug.

After a few moments, she mutters something about cleaning up and disappears into the bathroom.

"Is she on the rag?" Jason stage-whispers, cocking his thumb at the bathroom door.

"Dude, whatever you do, don't ever ask her that question."

"I know, Mika. I have the scars to remind me. Why do you think I'm asking you?"

"She's afraid for me, Jason, and she doesn't trust me anymore. I get it. I screwed that up, and I can't blame her. If the roles were reversed, I'd be scared too."

"Not like you're moving to fucking Alaska," he mumbles, and I grin. He's a good man, a great father, and a loving husband, who would do anything for his wife. He just doesn't handle emotion well, which is kind of funny, since he has twin daughters barreling toward puberty. He'll be drowning in emotions soon.

"THANKS FOR GIVING up your book club to come with me."

Sam turns to smile at me. "I hated this week's pick

anyway. The main character rubs me the wrong way, and I struggled through seven chapters before I tossed it aside. Not a shred of common sense in the woman."

I chuckle. Despite her meltdown in my kitchen a few days ago, Sam is generally a strictly no-nonsense, straightforward type. Almost abrasive at times, but her directness is what I love about her. What you see is what you get.

"Did you know they would be here?" she asks, tilting her head at a group converged in a corner of the large hospital atrium, partially repurposed for tonight's fundraising event.

"I figured." I shrug, casting a glance at the small clique of reporters fortunately focused on the current speaker. "This place is a genuine who's who of Boston, all in one location."

I wasn't going to come when I heard about the fund-raiser for the hospital's new transplant program. The program is geared toward improved post-transplant support both for the recipients and their families, as well as the families of the donors. I was actually approached to speak to the need for a more comprehensive aftercare program.

I get why I was asked. To have someone, who has been in the public eye, speak often carries—not necessarily justly—a little more weight. May loosen the purse strings. It's too raw for me still, and I politely declined.

Something made me want to come anyway. Maybe to challenge myself, I'm not sure. The hospital doesn't exactly hold good memories for me, but avoiding it would be cutting out the last nine months of Jamie's life. He spent a lot of time here at Tufts.

"Whoa," Sam whispers beside me. "Who's the giant bearded hottie?"

I follow her gaze. "Oh, that's Rick Porcello. He's a pitcher for the Red Sox." I give him a wave when he tilts his chin in my direction.

"Seriously?" Sam gasps. "You know him?"

"Well, yeah. I interviewed him a few times."

"How can you even form words around a guy like that?"

I laugh. The sensation still feels a little strange—rusty—but freeing as well. I used to laugh a lot. "Honey," I whisper in her ear. "He was half-naked at the time."

"Bullshit," she exclaims a little too loud, and a few heads swing in our direction.

"Hush. It's probably on YouTube somewhere. That was my job, Sam. I was in the locker room at most of their home games and some of the out-of-town ones. Trust me, when you're a sports journalist, you quickly get used to a roomful of very fit, naked men."

"Hell, I'd never get used to seeing *that*—" She nods at Porcello. "—in a towel."

"He only put that towel on for the interview," I tease her and am rewarded with an elbow in the ribs.

"Shut the front door!"

Again heads swivel, this time accompanied by irritated glares.

"You're drawing attention," I mumble, shoving her shoulder.

It's funny, all these years of working as a sports journalist for one of Boston's local networks, and Sam's never shown as much interest as now. Granted, sports have never been her thing, although she's always been supportive and proud of my career in the male-dominated field. Ironic she'd spark an interest now my career is effectively over.

I shouldn't be surprised; my friend has always had a healthy appreciation for beautiful men. She's happily married to a prime specimen herself, but in her own words, that doesn't render her blind.

I'm not exactly visually challenged myself, but a lot of

these guys are ten to twenty years younger than me and only bring out my strong maternal side.

I wince at my last thought. A maternal side I no longer have a use for.

"Is he an athlete too?" Sam asks; drawing me into the present as she indicates the small stage set up near the stairs.

A broad-shouldered, salt-and-pepper-haired man in an ill-fitting sports jacket steps up to the microphone.

"Not sure," I mumble, because something about him strikes me as very familiar.

Beside me Sam flips through the night's program, but my eyes narrow on the handsome stranger, trying to place him.

"Jude Parks? Is that familiar?" she asks, just as the same name is announced by the emcee.

I shake my head and watch as he walks up to the microphone.

"Good evening," he says after clearing his throat, looking decidedly uncomfortable when his dark eyes catch on mine. "A year and two months ago, our then eight-year-old daughter was diagnosed with acute cardiomyopathy. I won't bore you with the details, except to tell you that learning there's a timeline on your child's life is easily the worst night-mare imaginable for a parent."

His pained words touch me deeply and I feel an odd kinship with this man. I don't know him, but I feel his pain.

"Five months ago," he continues, and my breath stills in my throat. "Kelty received a new heart. A heart that shortly before it started pumping blood through my daughter's body had been beating in the chest of another child. The generosity of..."

I don't hear anymore, I'm already running for the exit.

Jude

I STRUGGLE through the rest of my prepared speech.

I'd noticed her when the woman she was standing beside barked out, "Bullshit," in the middle of the preceding speaker's presentation. A whole lot more put together than the first time I laid eyes on her, but unmistakably her.

I haven't forgotten her grief-marred face. Every so often, these past five months, I've wondered about her. My imagination conjuring up the different scenarios that might've caused her obvious pain.

For a month following Kelty's transplant, I'd often looked for her in the hospital's hallways. Almost eagerly wishing I'd encounter her again, but this time with a more hopeful expression. Maybe I'd simply caught her on a bad day, because the alternatives that came to mind were too painful to consider.

I'm not sure what made her suddenly run off, but it was difficult not to jump off the stage and take off after her. An irrational urge.

I'm a pretty laid-back guy who doesn't easily get riled or overly excited, yet it takes everything out of me to finish my presentation, receive my thanks, and step down to rejoin Cassie. We drove in together, while Mark stayed at home looking after our daughter.

"Are you okay?" she asks as she slides her arm in mine.

"Yeah, I just thought I recognized someone. You hungry?" I turn her to the buffet table set up with finger foods in an effort to distract her.

Not long after our daughter was discharged from the hospital, Mark and Cassie made the decision to sell their brownstone in Boston's Back Bay area and move to Chatham, just twenty minutes south of Orleans. It had been Mark's suggestion, which surprised me at first. Cassie explained they'd just found out she was pregnant a week before Kelty's surgery. They'd already discussed the possibility of moving away from the city with the new baby coming, but with Kelty's continued aftercare, Mark had started looking on Cape Cod. Since Mark is an author, who can work anywhere, and Cassie is an accountant, who's worked from home since Kelty was born, it doesn't really matter where they live.

The drive from their place to mine is only a scant twenty minutes and compared to the hour-and-a-half it was before, it has taken a lot of stress off all of us. We still have to drive into Boston for Kelty's appointments, but those will hopefully wind down to just a few visits a year over time.

"Seriously," Cassie, always observant, says through a mouthful of canapé. "Who was that woman? I saw you staring."

I should've known she'd notice. "I don't know her," I answer, shrugging my shoulders. "I bumped into her here once before."

Like I said, Cassie is observant, which is why she doesn't let me off the hook.

"Must've made an impression, then."

She has no idea.

Chapter Two

Jude

"DID YOU CHECK HER CREDENTIALS?"

I watch Kelty press her face to the glass of the aquarium as I'm checking in with Mandy.

Cassie just entered her third trimester, and at last check, her blood pressure was way too high, so she's on bed rest for the foreseeable future. That was a week ago, and since she's been homeschooling Kelty for the remainder of this school year—an infection at this point could spell disaster—I've taken over that task.

But after five months basically stuck indoors, my daughter is showing signs of cabin fever. Since my busy season doesn't really get into full swing until June, I figured we could get away for short day excursions and make it educational.

We did the Buttonwood Park Zoo in New Bedford two days ago, and today we're at the Woods Hole Science Aquarium, right here on the Cape.

For much of the past week I've handed off the reins to Mandy.

"I did, and get this, she wants to pay in advance for six months."

Alarm bells go off. It's not too common that folks want to pay ahead for a small, furnished vacation cottage, unless they have reason to stay under the radar. Vacation properties are hell to keep track of for authorities because of the frequent rental turnover.

"You sure she checks out?"

"Boss, trust me, she checks out."

I shake off the sense of foreboding and concede. "Okay then, fine, but if she turns out to be some drug peddler setting up shop for the season, or throws loud parties every night, I'll be looking at you to fix it."

The snort-giggles on the other side put a smile on my face. "You've got it, Boss."

"Anything else?"

"Nope, that's it. She's moving in tomorrow."

"I'll be at Tufts with Kelty," I point out.

"That's okay, I'll be here early, get her settled in."

As we've done on our earlier excursions, we head out for lunch after my princess has her fill of the aquarium. Lunches at my house consist of PB and J sandwiches, which is about the extent of my culinary skills. Daniel, the Cove Side Cooker's chef, takes care of our dinners at the restaurant.

"Find anything you like?" I ask Kelty, who is looking for nearby restaurants on my iPhone.

"Pie in the Sky Bakery," she suggests, with a mischievous grin I detect behind the protective mask we have her wear. She also carries around hand disinfectant, and by now, automatically squirts some in her hands when she's touched something that could spread germs. I hate she needs to worry about these things, but as Mark so astutely pointed out, she's not really worrying about it, if she does it by rote.

Mark has often been the voice of reason these past months when Cassie or I get a little too hyper-vigilant. It's hard not to do when risk is everywhere.

"The whole point of the exercise is to eat a healthy lunch, missy. Not sure pie qualifies," I point out.

Getting her to eat healthier while at my place continues to be a bit of a struggle. She eats healthy enough at Cassie's, but until she got sick, I mostly opted for easy fare. So the struggle is entirely my fault. I made do with fast food or stuff I could grab from the cereal shelf or the freezer section. Having not paid attention to a single nutritional label ever before, that adjustment to life after a transplant has been the most challenging for me. For someone who can barely boil water, it's a daunting responsibility. I happened to talk about this with Daniel when he took pity on me and offered his assistance.

"They don't just have pie, Dad. There's soups, and sandwiches with a side of salad. We could share a slice for dessert," she negotiates, something she's getting better at every damn day. "Besides," she hammers her point home. "Pie is made with fruit. Fruit is healthy."

I raise an eyebrow at her and don't bother mentioning the sugar, the flour, or the lard. She already knows.

"All right, Princess. Pie in the Sky it is. How far?" I cave, looking over to see her studying Google Maps.

"Down the street. You have to turn right out of the parking lot and just follow the road."

"I'm trusting you, honey," I tease her. "Your old man won't be happy if we end up in the drink."

The Tinker Bell giggle behind her mask is the best sound in the world, and I steal glances at my happy girl all the way to the bakery.

We end up taking the long way home and stop by Cassie and Mark's place to drop off a collection of baked goods.

"What's this?" Mark asks, taking in the boxes in my hands after giving Kelty a hug.

"Strawberry-rhubarb pie, cherry Danish, almond croissants, and cinnamon twirls," my daughter rattles off to Mark's amusement.

"Did you leave anything in the store?" he asks, stepping aside for us to come in.

"I wanted to get the pecan pie as well, and they had chocolate chip muffins, but Daddy said it was enough."

"I'd say. I hope you guys are taking at least half of that home, because we'll never be able to finish it."

"No silly," Kelty grins. "We have our own in the truck." Before I have a chance to say anything in my defense at Mark's raised eyebrows, she changes topics. "Is Mom awake? Can I go see her?"

"Not sure, just peek around the corner first, okay?"

The moment she disappears up the stairs, Mark turns a teasing grin on me. "You're such a pushover, Parks."

I shrug a little sheepishly. "I told her she could pick everyone's favorites. I just didn't realize she meant Daniel, Amanda, and the rest of the crew at the restaurant as well. She was having a blast, I didn't have the heart to be a wet rag."

"Must've cost a whack." He chuckles at my wince.

"Maybe," I admit. "But it was worth every penny to see her smile all the way home."

Mika

. . .

"THERE'S a laundry facility in the restaurant and at the main house. I'm sure the boss won't mind you running a load from time to time."

The perky brunette was waiting for me outside of the Cape Cod style, shingled cottage. Sitting on the picnic table, she was drinking from a Starbucks cup and enjoying the morning sun. Mandy introduced herself as the person I'd been talking to on the phone, and that her boss sends his regrets, but he's up in Boston for the day on a personal matter.

I follow her into the cottage and am surprised when it actually looks like the pictures on the Airbnb listing. Of course with the wide-angle lens it looked a little bigger, but I'm really pleased with the place. The big room at the front is open concept, with a kitchen and dining room to the left of the front door, and a sitting area on the right with three doors in the back wall. The one on the right leads to a decent-sized bedroom with a queen-sized bed. The one on the far left to what looks to be a newly renovated bathroom.

"That would be awesome," I answer her. "But if not, it's not a big deal. I saw a Laundromat as I came through town as well. Either way, I should be okay."

Mandy pulls open the center door open to reveal half of it a storage closet with cleaning supplies, and the other half serves as a scarcely stocked linen closet. "Fuck."

"Excuse me?"

"Not you—*this*." She points at the closet. "Last year, toward the end of the season, we had it restocked with extra sheets and towels and now half of them are gone already. We've had all of four guests in here so far this year. People are assholes."

I'm not going to argue with that, since in large lines I

agree with her. People *are* assholes. "I can always pick up some—"

She dismisses me with a wave of her hand. "You pay for extra sheets and towels to be included, you're getting sheets and towels. Leave it to me." She closes the linen closet and walks to the door, looking over her shoulder at me. "Well, come on, I assume you've got bags that need bringing in?"

Looks like Mandy also doubles as bellhop. I actually find I like the younger woman. She reminds me a bit of Sam with her direct manner, although Sam is perhaps a little more refined.

She's already waiting by my new—to me—white Subaru Outback, the back of which is jam-packed. It probably would've been easier in the SUV, but I traded it in for this newer and more fuel economic wagon just last week.

All in the spirit of a fresh start.

Okay, fine, in the spirit of conserving funds as well. Not that I'm hurting—not yet anyway—but at this point, I'm not even sure if I want to stay in journalism. My objective is to downscale and simplify. Life as a journalist is far from simple.

Until my house in Boston is sold, I'm on a strict budget, and I have to find a job, but that's for another day. Today I settle into my new surroundings.

I join Mandy by my car and lift the gate.

"Holy shit. You really are settling in," she says, catching my Keurig machine as it comes tumbling down from the top of the pile. "We do have a coffeemaker, you know," she teases, grabbing the bulk-sized box of K-Cup pods next.

"I'm a sucker for freshly brewed," I confess, dislodging the laundry basket with groceries I pulled from my pantry at the last minute. "And I don't like waste."

"I can tell," Mandy mumbles, climbing up the steps in front of me.

It takes us almost half an hour to empty the back of the Subaru. Mandy is trying to find room to put away the groceries, while I stand in the middle of the living room, surveying the disaster in the once sparse space. Boxes, suitcases, baskets, a couple of lamps, my laptop and cameras, and two garment bags holding my work clothes. I might as well have stuffed them in a box since they ended up rumpled underneath the groceries.

"Those all clothes?" Mandy asks, pointing at the bags and suitcases.

"Mmmm."

"Sheeet, girl. Where do you plan to sleep? You've got a small built-in closet and a three-drawer dresser." She waves at my stuff in the living room. "This here requires a two hundred square foot walk-in closet."

"It's not so bad," I mutter, mostly trying to convince myself.

When Sam saw me packing all my clothes, she'd laughed at me as well. Aside from my casual clothes, in my line of work you need to have a decent selection of professional outfits available. Can't appear on camera in the same getup too often. Of course that still doesn't explain why I felt the need to lug all of them to a waterside cottage on Cape Cod. Not like I'd have use for any of them here.

Maybe it's because my wardrobe is the only thing that was just mine from my old life. Everything else was either a remnant of my former marriage or held strong reminders of Jamie. I look around at my boxes of books and photographs, and the two lamps I bought just last year for my bedroom, and realize how true that is. Aside from my picture albums, there is no indication there was ever anyone more than me.

I promptly burst out in tears.

"Oh good Lord. Jesus have mercy. Christ, girl, don't cry. I was just kidding." She runs into the bathroom and comes back with a roll of toilet paper and shoves it in my hands. "Bastards took the boxes of tissues too," she mumbles, and I promptly start laughing while the tears still roll down my face.

"I'm s-sorry," I stammer, equal parts embarrassed and mortified, but for some damn reason I'm still giggling like a hyena. Hysteria, that's got to be it. I've officially gone bonkers. With Herculean effort, I manage to get myself under control. "I've had a tough few months and it's all kind of landing on me now."

"Right. Well then, I hope you don't get me the wrong way or anything, but..." Instead of finishing her sentence, I'm startled when Mandy unexpectedly wraps me up in a hug, squeezing me tight before awkwardly letting me go. "You looked like you needed one."

"Thanks," I mutter stupidly. What else can you say? "I, uh, I guess I did need that," I admit, finding my slightly hysterical outburst has vanished as fast as it appeared.

"Anytime. Never was much good at giving advice or anything, but I do give good hugs."

"You sure do," I agree with a small smile.

I HAVEN'T SEEN Mandy since she left for the restaurant, inviting me to come grab a bite whenever I want. Instead I opted to putter around the cottage.

Between the closet and dresser I was only able to store half of what I brought, so after stacking my books on top of the dresser—I might have to pick up a shelving unit somewhere for those—I stuff the boxes with clothes and shoes I don't see myself wearing anytime soon.

Unsure of what to do with them, I carry the boxes out to the car for now, and drive into town in search of a grocery store to pick up some necessities and food for the next week. I fully intend to take some time to explore later, and at least won't have to worry about groceries.

A black SUV is parked in the driveway by the main house, on the other side of the small restaurant parking lot, by the time I get back. The owner must be back.

For a moment I'm tempted to go introduce myself, but when my stomach starts growling—I haven't really eaten since breakfast—I carry my groceries inside and make myself a quick sandwich.

Armed with a plate and my favorite travel mug with decaf, I head outside. On the small front deck, with a wooden bench and small side table, I eat my dinner with my feet propped up on the railing.

It's my first opportunity to take in my surroundings. It's a beautiful piece of property bordering on the cove and far enough removed from the road so you barely hear passing traffic. All three buildings—the cottage, the restaurant, and the two-story home—have dark gray, wood shingle siding. The restaurant is literally on the water's edge, with a large patio deck that partially overhangs the water, held up by a structure of pillars and beams. I imagine, once the weather gets a little warmer that will be the perfect place to dine. Both the house and the cottage are set back a little. If you look at the property from the main driveway, the restaurant would be in the middle, which means that even set back a bit from the water, my view ahead is mostly unobstructed.

It's gorgeous, with the sun dropping lower in the sky, deepening the colors around me. I can't wait to see what it looks like during a sunrise. I'm tempted to set an alarm so I don't miss it.

"Hi."

I turn my head to the parking lot and find a pretty little girl with light blonde hair, maybe eight or nine, walking my way. For a second I have a hard time answering.

"Hello," I finally manage.

"Have you seen our heron?" she asks, stopping to look at the water's edge, her eyes squinting against the setting sun. I automatically follow suit.

"No. I've sat here for a while, but I haven't seen one. Do you see it often?"

I look over and find she's come around the front and lowers herself on the step. "It's a great white heron," she informs me in her melodic singsong voice, keeping her eyes focused on the water. "There are lots of blue herons around, the white herons are more rare, but there's one who comes here at night to fish."

"I don't think I've ever seen a white heron," I admit, following her gaze out on the cove.

"Princess!"

My eyes dart to the main house. All I can see is a pair of arms braced on the railing of the porch. The rest of the man's body isn't visible.

"Coming!" the girl yells back, getting up from her perch on my steps. She turns to me. "I have to go."

"Okay, honey. I'm gonna sit here for a little longer. I'll keep my eye open for your heron."

Instead of doing that, I follow the girl's bouncing blonde hair as she crosses the parking lot to the main house.

Chapter Three

Jude

"Jude!"

I'm working in the small office in the back of the restaurant, when Daniel calls out.

"Yeah!"

"Got a minute?"

I push back from the desk and go find him. I don't mind the distraction. I've been trying to make headway with the piles of paperwork I'm still digging my way through. I have to find a better system than 'when I have a minute,' which worked before my daughter got sick, but not so much since and certainly not now she's staying with me.

I find him in the kitchen, trying to stop a spreading puddle of water coming out from under the industrial dishwasher.

"Fuck, man. Again?" I rush back into the hall where a panel in the floor opens up to the water shut-off valve.

Don't ask me why the hell someone would put it there.

The original building went up in the late 1800s, but since then it's been added on to and electrical and plumbing were installed. The structure itself has withstood time, but some of the later 'improvements' have had to be redone. Not a lot of space to do it in either. There's a small cellar under the bar in the restaurant—with just room for some of the more vintage wines—and the crawlspace accessible from the hall, so whatever upgrades I'd want to make would mean major disruptions. Not something I'd even consider at the start of the season.

I walk back into the kitchen. "Same problem?" I ask, helping Daniel empty out the dirty dishes and stacking them in the tub sink so we can have a look.

"Could well be. Turned it on, started on prep, and the next thing I know there's water all over the place."

"That's what Mandy says happened last time. It's gotta be a seal or something. Help me pull it out," I instruct him, hoping it's just a loose hose.

Daniel is a burly guy with a big, russet beard. If not for the hairnet keeping that beard in check, he'd look more like a fisherman than a chef.

It takes a bit of elbow grease and a chorus of grunts, but between us we manage to pull the heavy appliance away from the wall. The seal between the hose and our water supply seems intact.

"Well, shit," Daniel comments, twisting the hose to show a crack running all the way back into the bowels of the dishwasher.

"Great way to start the day," I complain, getting to my feet and brushing uselessly at my damp knees. "Get this mess cleaned up and I'll give customer service a call. The damn thing isn't even three years old. At least it should fall under warranty. Looks like we're back to doing dishes by hand."

"Tell them to bring a damn replacement," Daniel suggests. "Second time in as many months. Can't run a restaurant if this keeps happening."

It takes me half an hour on the phone; quickly dismissing the less than helpful guy in customer service, not getting anywhere with the service rep he connects me to, and finally ending up with a supervisor. That guy is a little more forthcoming, especially after my threat to drag his company through the mud at the biannual Chamber of Commerce meeting in Hyannis in two weeks.

He ends up promising a replacement will be installed by start of business Saturday. Sadly that means we not only have dish duty today, but tomorrow as well.

My next calls are to see how many additional hands we can get in here to absorb the extra work this'll create. Not the way I want to kick off the new season.

By the time Mandy sticks her head into my office, I have my elbows on my desk and my head in my hands.

"Trouble, Boss?"

"Fucking dishwasher," I grunt by way of explanation. "And I can't get any of the spares we have on the list to come in."

I'd be washing dishes myself if I didn't have my daughter to look after. She hangs around the restaurant often enough during the day, but we spend our nights at home. That time with her is sacred. I guess I could always drop her with Cassie and Mark for the night, but that would defeat the purpose of her staying with me.

"Is your sister in town?" I ask Mandy. She's a student and has helped out before during busy summer months when she's back on the Cape.

"Naw, Becca is still in Philly. She's got a boyfriend now, so she's staying there."

"Fuck. I need an extra pair of hands."

Mandy looks like a light just went off in her head, and her face cracks in a smile. "Leave it to me. I'll figure it out."

I don't even ask. If she says she'll find a way, she will. Granted, I may end up with her eighty-year-old Aunt Meida in my kitchen, but I'll take that chance.

"Great. I'm gonna go check on my daughter."

I'd installed her in the restaurant dining room with her schoolwork this morning, while I tried to get some work done, and occasionally poked my head in to see how she was doing. I haven't checked in a while.

The dining room is empty; her books and backpack no longer there. She must've gone up to the house to put her stuff away.

"She said she was done," Mandy says, having followed me into the restaurant. "She's probably over at the cottage chatting up that reporter chick."

"Reporter chick?" I echo, confused to say the least.

"Your new tenant? Didn't I tell you? It's Mika Spencer." At my blank face she rolls her eyes. "*Boston Sports News*? Christ, Boss, you really need to start paying attention."

I've never been one to follow sports that closely. Oh, I like watching a good game as much as any other guy—I even have my favorite teams—I'm just not interested in all the media hype around them.

I have no idea what a well-known sports reporter is doing roughing it in my rental cottage and frankly, it's none of my business. My daughter hanging out with her *is* my business, which is why I head out after her, making time I don't really have to get acquainted with my new tenant.

I'm just crossing the parking lot when I hear Kelty's voice.

"Dad! I'm over here."

I look up to find her on the steps of the cottage; next to the new tenant I haven't had a chance to introduce myself to. The first glimpse I get of the blonde sitting beside my daughter knocks all the air from my chest.

———

Mika

I LOOK up from the digital display on my camera, when the little girl calls out.

Her white heron hadn't showed last night, but this morning—when I was sitting on the bench, covered in a blanket enjoying my coffee and the sunrise—I saw him fly in. I rushed inside, grabbed one of my cameras and started snapping photos.

He was majestic, standing silently along the water's edge in the morning light, his head slightly bent scanning for food. Every now and then he'd dart down, fast as lighting, his head disappearing in the water. When he'd come up, flinging water droplets back, I could almost see the muscles of his long sleek neck working whatever fish or frog was unlucky enough to cross his path.

When the girl showed up on my doorstep just now, I quickly grabbed the camera to show her.

My eyes catch on the man she called out to, and before I realize it I'm on my feet, my heart pounding in my chest. Those dark eyes looking as shocked as I feel.

Whatever higher force is at play here is a cruel bitch.

"Dad, you should see the pictures of the heron." She jumps up when her father approaches.

With each of his long purposeful strides his smile gets bigger, as does my urge to run.

"You look familiar," he says when he reaches us. His voice gritty but warm. Exactly how I remember it. "Jude Parks."

"I get that a lot," I answer by rote, but it seems to take him aback. "In my line of work," I add, and now understanding floods his features as I take his offered hand. "Mika Spencer."

"Right, yes, Mandy mentioned we have a resident celebrity, but I have to confess, I had no clue who she was talking about. I recognize you from the two times I saw you at Tufts."

"You were at the hospital?" his daughter pipes up in her musical voice, and I suddenly freeze as the full weight of this situation lands on me.

My God.

"And I see you've met my daughter, Kelty."

A pretty name for a precious girl. I just hadn't realized how precious until now. I resort to nodding, since I can't trust my voice.

"Can you show Dad the heron?" Kelty asks.

I pull up the images on my digital display; eager to cover the fact I haven't yet answered her earlier question. "Sure."

I force every thought and emotion into a tight box, to be examined at a later time. Not now.

Stepping down from the porch, I hold the camera display turned to him as I scroll through the images.

"Show him the one with the sparkly water drops," she suggests.

I tilt the screen my way to find the series of shots she's talking about, and feel her father take a step closer to peer over my shoulder.

"Those are beautiful. Are you a professional photographer too?" he asks, and I suppress a shiver at his proximity. It's like every cell in my body is acutely aware of him.

"It's just a hobby."

"One with professional results," he counters. "I should know, I've been looking for some decent artwork for the restaurant that captures the true spirit of the cove for months now. Anything that even comes close is priced out of the stratosphere."

"Thanks, I guess," I mumble, not quite sure what to do with the compliment. "I just do it for fun."

"I'm just saying," he emphasizes. "If you didn't already have an exciting career, you could easily make one of this."

No one—least of all me—has ever looked at my photography as anything other than a way to pass the time. Weird that it would take a stranger to see the opportunity. It certainly wouldn't have occurred to me.

It's on my lips to explain I no longer have the career he refers to, but I don't want to open up any more than I already have.

"Thanks," I repeat instead.

"We should get out of your hair. We need to eat lunch and then it's nap time for Kelty, and—"

"Dad!"

"What?"

"It's embarrassing." His daughter glares at him, her button mouth set in a stubborn line.

"What's embarrassing?"

I almost chuckle at the clueless, yet exasperated, expression on his face.

"Naps are for toddlers," she whines, the stubborn line morphing into an adorable pout.

"Naps are for people of all ages who are still recovering," he counters.

I know I shouldn't wade in, but I can't help myself.

"Naps are also for people who need their beauty sleep—like the one I'm about to have."

"Come on, Princess. You heard the woman, she needs her beauty sleep."

This time when her father gives her a little nudge, Kelty doesn't argue.

"Later!" the girl yells out when they cross the parking lot.

"You bet," I call back, wondering how the fuck it is I ended up here.

"I'M DOING GREAT, SAM."

I lie. I'm not,

I'm shaken to the core, but I haven't had time to process things yet. For now I'm on a mission to find out why it is my best friend suggested this place.

"I was asking how you knew about this place?"

"I don't. Not really," Sam responds.

"Well, you're the one who suggested it."

"My brother did. It's one of his summer listings, and he said he knows the owner personally. According to him the place is great. Why? Is there something wrong with it?"

Her brother has been a real estate agent on the Cape for many years. It never occurred to ask his help when I started looking.

"Nothing. The cottage is small, but I love it. There's nothing wrong with it, except..."

When I finish explaining the situation it's quiet for a moment, but then she lets it fly.

"You have *got* to be kidding me!"
Nope.
No kidding here.
I wish I were.

Chapter Four

Mika

THIS MORNING IS as peaceful as yesterday's was.

The only difference is I was well rested yesterday, but barely got any sleep last night. The need for coffee is high, especially since I'd planned to head down to the end of the Cape this morning to check out Provincetown.

It's shameful that I've lived in and around Boston most of my life, have traveled all over the U.S. and overseas, but have never visited Provincetown. It's at the northern tip of the Cape and apparently not only a historically significant location, but also a beacon of diversity, and a quaint, artsy community.

That was the plan, but after flopping around my bed all night, trying to come to terms with my current predicament, I'm not so sure.

Finding out who the little girl is was a shock. A big one. Feeling the strong visceral draw to her father was another. The fact I ended up moving in right next door to them is beyond casual happenstance. And right now, that's what I'm struggling with most.

If I hadn't had a chance to interact with Kelty before I found out, I would've packed my bags and left. Knowing what I know, I shouldn't be here, but the girl had already made as much of an impression on me as her father had.

It's seriously freaky, definitely wrong, and has my stomach twisted in knots. So why is it that instead of leaving, I sit here in the early morning hours staring at their house for even just a glimpse of either one of them, like some obsessed stalker?

How would I even explain this situation? I can only imagine what Jude might think if I tell him. He'll never believe my being here is completely coincidental. I wouldn't, if I were in his shoes. How is it possible to rationalize being here, for not even two days, has given me a deeper sense of human connection—a clearer sense of purpose—than I've felt in the past almost six months?

I don't even understand it myself.

———

MY HEAD IS a bit clearer after my second cup, some breakfast, and a refreshing shower, but Provincetown will have to wait for another day.

While munching on a bagel, I was checking the classifieds online for job postings, when I bumped into an ad for an estate sale. The house is actually right across the cove near Weeset Point.

When Sam and I were students, we'd sometimes go to estate sales. Not that we had money to buy anything, but it was kind of interesting to see how the other half lived. Seeing that ad reminded me of those times when, in hindsight, our worries were so simple.

I stick my feet in a pair of flip-flops, grab my camera and purse, and head outside where Mandy is just coming up the steps.

"Morning."

"Hey, Mandy." I smile at her.

"You heading out somewhere?"

"An estate sale."

She nods. "William Bentley's place off Tonset? Yeah, I saw that. I hear his kids wanna sell the place. It's worth a sweet penny these days. You looking for anything special?"

"Not really, although a bookshelf would come in handy. Maybe I'll drive around a bit. Get a little taste of life in Orleans." I chuckle. "If I'm lucky, maybe find a job."

Mandy's eyes light up at my last comment. "Yeah? You're looking for work? Well, it just so happens…"

Five minutes later, I pull out on the road heading into town. Cove Side Cooker's new kitchen help.

What can I say, Mandy is very convincing. I'm not sure how much she knows about my history—I'm sure most of it is readily available online—but she sure knows what buttons to push. She pointed out since the job is part time, I'd still have time to explore. I'll be working in the kitchen, which will minimize the risk of recognition, and her coup de grâce was that I'll save on gas since it's within convenient walking distance. I had to laugh at that last one.

As I drive around the cove, I ignore the pangs of guilt, and tell myself the fortuitous job offer is perhaps a sign I'm right where I'm supposed to be. At least for the coming months.

The house is easy to find. It sits on a rise in the otherwise mostly level landscape, overlooking the water. Another prime example of Cape Cod architecture with the signature wood shingle siding and white trim. Except this place is massive.

I realize pretty quickly I'm a little out of my league. The driveway is lined with cube vans and trucks sporting company names on the side, and most of the crowd roaming through the house appears to be here in professional capacity.

I stop at a collection of sea glass displayed on a small side table and wonder if that was all found locally. I wouldn't mind scouring the beach at low tide to see what I can pick up. Might be good exercise. I haven't really worked out in a long time; maybe beach walks will help me get back in shape.

"Find anything you like?"

I swing around to find Jude right behind me. "Oh, hey. I'm not actually looking, just…browsing. What are you doing here?"

He grins and shrugs. "Was hoping to find a bookcase."

I'm not sure what Mandy is playing at, but she clearly has a big mouth.

Jude

"OH."

She looks as stunned as she did yesterday.

She recognized me, that much was clear, but I wasn't so sure she was happy to see me. Granted, especially the first time in the hallway at Tufts was not something she'd fondly remember. She'd been a mess. A beautiful mess, but still. Then earlier this month she ran when she saw me in the lobby. At least I think that's why. She looked right at me and bailed.

I was floored when I saw her sitting on the steps of my rental with Kelty. What are the odds? She did seem a bit uncomfortable, so even though I would've loved to stay and learn a little more about her, I took my reluctant daughter home instead. It's not like there's a hurry: Ms. Spencer has paid up front 'til the end of October. Plenty of time.

Then Mandy stuck her head into my office earlier to let me know our tenant needs a bookcase, and exactly where she went to find one. I didn't miss the mischievous glint in her eyes when I asked her to keep an eye on Kelty.

Mika Spencer. I looked her up last night. Shocked at the pages and pages of search results that came up. The woman even has a Wikipedia page. I wasn't exactly snooping, just getting a lay of the land. Seeing the way she looks in her publicity photos, I realize I have probably seen her before in the media. I just didn't connect the tied-back hair, flawless makeup, and professional smile to the disheveled, emotional woman I'd bumped into.

"Mandy sent you, didn't she?" she asks, a wry smile on her face.

"Yup. She's very protective of me," I joke.

"Of you? How so?"

"She guards my reputation. Doesn't want it spread on *TripAdvisor* I'm a cheap host and don't provide my guests with the basic necessities."

"A bookcase is hardly a basic necessity in a vacation cottage," she counters with a faint, amused smile.

"Depends on your point of view." I lightly put my hand on her elbow and start walking into the next room. "For instance, my daughter's stepfather would strongly disagree. Books are as important as breathing to him." At her puzzled look, I add, "He's an author."

Her eyes light up. "Really? What's his name? I love to read."

"Mark Sommer, he—"

She rips her elbow from my hand and swings around her mouth open in a perfect O. "Get out! I have four of his books in my bedroom. I love him."

Not sure if it's her obvious excitement at Mark's name, the fact she keeps his books in the sanctuary of her bedroom, or her heartfelt declaration, but it immediately sours my mood.

"He's okay," I grumble. "He's also about to become a father. He and Kelty's mom are having a baby."

Don't ask me why I find it necessary to share that information. Still, I glance over to see her reaction.

"Your daughter must be so excited." Her smile is warm and genuine, and the momentary tightness in my shoulders relaxes.

"She is. She's also very impatient. Cassie—that's her mom—was put on strict bed rest, which is why Kelty is staying with me."

"Does she normally live with them?"

"Excuse me." A somewhat disgruntled man, armed with a clipboard and tape measure, tries to get into the room we're blocking. I step aside, pulling Mika with me.

"Used to, yes. They were in Boston before; she had her friends and school there. She'd spend more time here during the summers."

"They're not in Boston anymore?"

"No. They moved here when…" I stop myself from sharing more. It seems insensitive to talk about a time that was happy for us, but not so happy for her. She'd looked wrecked on the day I met her. "When they found out about the baby," I conclude.

I keep my hand loosely around her elbow—trying not to stroke my thumb over the soft skin on the inside of her arm—as we stroll around the Bentley house in search of a bookcase.

"That one's nice." I point at a large cabinet with glass doors, holding a collection of old books.

"It is. Perhaps a little big, though," she says, hiding a smile. "Unless you have room in your house, because I don't think it would fit in the cottage. I don't even think you could get it through the door."

She's right, it wouldn't. We find another in the next room, similar, but instead of seven or eight feet tall, this one is at eye level for me.

"It's pretty," she comments, peeking at the tag hanging off a knob. "But you know a plain shelving unit would do just as well, right? It's kind of expensive," she adds on a whisper.

Half an hour later, I have the cabinet strapped down and loaded in the back of my Traverse, and am leaning against the gate.

"Where to next?" I ask, cutting off the ongoing argument about who should be paying for the bookcase.

She throws me an irritated look, but I bite off a grin when she rolls her eyes and answers my question. "I was heading for the beach. I brought my camera. When is low tide?"

"Not sure, but it changes from day-to-day. Why low tide?" I pull out my phone and look up Nauset Beach tides.

"I saw some sea glass in there." I remember she was looking at some when I found her. "I want to see if I can find any."

"It says low tide was at ten thirty. It's near noon now; it takes six hours, give or take, to peak. You should still have plenty of beach left."

"What about the cabinet?"

44

"It's not that heavy. I can have it set up for you by the time you get back, if you want."

"If you're sure."

"Absolutely." I push away from the truck. "Go explore, make some more pretty pictures."

Her smile hits me in the midsection and she gives me a little wave as she walks over to her wagon. I'm tempted to follow her to the beach, but I have a kid and a restaurant waiting at home.

Besides, there's something I want to do first.

I JUST DROPPED Kelty off in Chatham with Mark and Cassie, where she'll be spending the weekend.

It's Memorial Day weekend, the unofficial beginning of the season. Summer may not officially start for another three and a half weeks, but there are a lot of folks who prefer the relative quiet of the Cape before schools let out for the summer.

When I pull into the driveway, I notice there are already quite a few cars in the parking lot. I also see Mika must've returned while I was out. Too bad I don't have time to check in with her.

I put the bookcase against the sidewall of the living area, flipping the loveseat to the other side, so now when you walk in the sitting area is better defined. I like it; I just hope she does.

"We've got a party of twelve wanting to come in at seven," Mandy announces, the phone pressed to her chest when I walk in.

"Jesus." I look around the almost full restaurant. "Too cold for the deck."

"Actually, it's pretty nice out there."

"Until the sun goes down," I remind her. It cools down fast when you're on the water.

"We could set up the heaters. Why don't I ask them?"

I nod. We have five patio heaters we often set up at the end of the season. People aren't ready to let go of summer yet, despite it getting pretty cool at night toward the end of September. It wouldn't take much to set a couple up.

"They're good sitting outside," she says, adding their reservation on the whiteboard.

"Do you have enough hands on the floor?"

"Yup. We're good for now."

"All right, I guess I'll go help out in the kitchen. Hope they come through with that delivery tomorrow."

I'm about to push through the doors that separate the kitchen from the restaurant when Mandy calls out.

"Boss, forgot to mention; I got us some extra help."

Chapter Five

Mika

"SORRY."

I look up as Penny comes into the kitchen with another tub of dirty dishes. I haven't even finished the previous one. She looks a little guilty so I send her a reassuring smile.

Mandy introduced Penny and Trish when I came in around five. Both local women, apparently. Penny is the younger of the two, probably early thirties, if that. Trish looks to have a few years on me and is the more reserved of the two.

Then Mandy took me into the kitchen where I met Daniel, the chef, and his sous chef, Melissa. When she'd mentioned helping out in the kitchen, I'm not sure what I expected. I thought I might be assisting with prep, doing a little cleanup, and maybe plate, but instead I was installed at the huge tub sink where large stacks of dirty dishes were already waiting.

To say I hit the floor running might be an understatement.

I've been scrubbing for what feels like hours and can't seem to make a dent in the dishes Trish and Penny keep adding to.

Daniel hasn't said much, but Melissa seems nice. She's the one who explained why I should prioritize cookware before cutlery, and cutlery before dishes. She also suggested I take the racks from the broken dishwasher and use them as drying racks. Every so often Melissa clears the dried dishes and the other half of the counter is freed up again. Everyone's part in the operation runs smoothly, but I appear to be the rusty cog in the wheel.

I can't help chuckle. This is not what I envisioned when I said I was looking for work. Still, it's not particularly mentally taxing, and allows for my mind to drift.

When I came back around three this afternoon, Jude's truck had been gone, but I could see he'd been there. The gorgeous, glass door bookcase features prominently in the living room, and I love how it looks filled with my books. He moved the furniture around a little and it immediately felt more personal and homey coming in the door.

What caught me off-guard was the flat glass bowl filled with sea glass. I recognized some of the pieces; it was the same glass I'd been eyeing at the estate sale. That was surprisingly thoughtful. It's also evidence he pays attention, and let's be honest, that's not always a quality evident in the opposite gender. At least not in many men I've known.

I rinsed off the few smooth-worn shards of colored glass I found, added them to the collection, and quickly uploaded the shots I took to the laptop. There hadn't been time left to have a good selective look at them, because Mandy was expecting me at the Cooker for five.

"Never seen anyone smile like that over dishes. Penny for your thoughts?"

In contrast to Jude's almost rough voice, Daniel's is

surprisingly smooth and cultured. You'd think it would be the reverse.

I shake my head, grinning. "I'm not thinking of dishes, that's for sure."

He leans his hip against the counter and crosses his arms over his wide chest. "Ah, come on. You're not sharing?"

I recognize the flirting. Not like I haven't been subjected to my share in my career. It was almost par for the course, and mostly from men too young for me, who thought they could avoid difficult questions by trying to rattle me. They learned quickly I couldn't be rattled. Not by them anyway.

Daniel's handsome in a giant ginger teddy bear way, probably closer to my age, and isn't holding back information I want to get at, so I let myself be tempted into a little harmless back-and-forth.

"There are some things a girl doesn't share."

"You know that's cruel, right?" he teases. "Now my imagination will have to fill in the blanks and I won't sleep all night."

Melissa snorts from somewhere behind him. "Don't mind him," she advises. "The lumbering fool is still honing his skills in the fine art of seduction. I'll give it to you though; you're still standing here when most would've run for the door from one look at his ugly mug. Good thing the man can cook, it's his one redeeming grace."

"She's just jealous," Daniel retorts, without so much as a glance at her but with a wink for me. "She's wanted a piece of this…" He runs his big paws up and down his thick torso. "…since the first time she met me."

It's obvious this is a well-rehearsed spiel between the two. It's warm, and reminds me of the bickering Sam and her brother, Steve, would get into.

"Any reason you're hitting on the new help instead of getting me my surf and turf platter for table fourteen?"

The question is clearly for Daniel, but I still turn my head at the sound of Jude's gruff voice to find him standing in the doorway. The moment I do, his eyes go big.

"Mika? What are you doing here?"

"I'm the new help." I shrug, but I've already lost his attention, since he turns an angry glare on Daniel.

"In that case, you really want to get back behind the stove," he tells the other man in a deceptively calm voice. Melissa snorts again, and Daniel lifts his hands defensively and backs away from my sink, the flash of white teeth in his beard betraying a smile.

"So that's the way the wind's blowing," I hear him mumble before he adds out loud, "Surf and turf for fourteen coming up."

With one last glance at me, Jude walks out of the kitchen to Daniel's deep chuckle.

I keep to my own thoughts after that, listening to the occasional comfortable banter from the two chefs with half an ear. The tedium of washing dishes allows my mind to drift, and I realize for the first time in a long while, I'm almost content.

However, much later when Mandy walks in with the last tub of dishes from the dining room, my feet are aching and my hands are red and swollen from being in hot water all night. The kitchen is officially closed, Melissa and Daniel disappeared, and I'm just finishing up the last of the pots and utensils.

"I'll do this last batch, go take the load off. They're in the bar having a night cap."

I nod and smile my thanks before drying my hands, removing the apron, and heading into the restaurant, where I find Trish, Melissa, and Daniel sitting at the bar Jude appears to be manning.

"What's your poison?" he asks, when he sees me dragging my ass in.

"I think I'll pass." I direct a tired smile at the group. "I'm afraid if I have a drink I won't be able to make it home at all."

"I'll walk you home," Daniel says, getting up from his stool.

"There's no need, I—"

"Sit your ass down, Daniel," Jude snaps, cutting me off as he rounds the bar and takes my elbow. Before I can even launch a protest, I'm being led out the door, the sound of snickering behind me.

Jude

FUCKING DANIEL.

And *fucking* Mandy.

Jesus.

I'm seriously considering looking for a new set of friends.

What the hell was Mandy thinking putting that woman on dishwashing duty? Within easy reach of our resident tomcat, who clearly was already on the prowl. *Christ.*

Mika half-stumbles and I'm just able to grab her arm to keep her from falling.

"Careful."

"Then don't run," she snaps, yanking her arm from my hold. "I can't even see where the hell I'm going."

"You should've left your porch light on," I grumble.

When the kitchen closes we usually shut off the parking lot lights to discourage latecomers from pulling in, but it makes visibility poor.

"Don't worry, I will next time," she says, almost taking a nosedive when she trips over the last porch step.

"Why?" I ask, stopping at the bottom, looking up at her.

"Why what?"

"Why would you take a job washing dishes?"

She turns her back to me and opens the door, stepping inside. Probably still pissed. I can't really blame her. I'm acting like an angry bear. Then she surprises me when the porch light turns on and she steps back outside. "First of all," she starts, sitting down on the top step. "I was given the impression I'd be helping in the kitchen." She seems to think about that for a moment before she adds, "Which I guess wasn't technically a lie. I just thought it would be more...varied."

I sit down on the bottom step, twisting my body so I can keep looking at her. "Guess Mandy roped you in?" Her nod confirms it. "We had a flood in the kitchen yesterday morning when the dishwasher crapped out. Again. We should have a replacement tomorrow morning," I explain, before pushing her a bit more. "But why take on a job you're way overqualified for? Are you in trouble?" The mere thought she might be is causing a feeling of unease. A need to protect her from whatever had her run to the Cape to hide out. Because that's the conclusion I've come to. It's the only thing that makes sense when someone with—by all accounts—a successful and public career rents a two-bedroom cottage in some out-of-the-way place, and takes on a job washing dishes in a restaurant. I know something bad happened to her last December—and I'm sure I can find out what if I dig deeper in all the links my Google search spit out when I put in her name—but I'd much rather she tell me herself than read it in online gossip.

"I'm not in trouble," she says earnestly, lifting her eyes to look out at the moon bouncing off the water. A breath, I wasn't aware I was holding, releases in an audible exhale. She grins and turns back to me. "You thought I was on the lam?"

I shrug a little self-consciously. "It was one of the possibilities. It seems obvious you're hiding from something."

"In some ways, maybe. Steering clear of public scrutiny for sure, but mostly I'm hoping to find something."

"What are you looking for?" I ask, and I sense, without intending it to be, my question is a hard one. She takes her time, letting her gaze drift off in the distance. I don't want to push, and I'm not in a hurry, so I quietly wait for her to talk.

"Me," she finally says without meeting my eyes. "I've been…lost, I guess is the best way to describe it. One minute you think you're doing okay and then suddenly find yourself defined by circumstances. By what you do—or worse, by what happened to you—rather than by who you are. It's no one's fault, really. Stuff happens. Your life looks to be on track until suddenly it isn't, and you've lost sight of how you fit in."

"I think I understand what you're saying, to some extent," I offer cautiously. "We delude ourselves into a sense of control, until something happens to change the very core of that belief. Something that completely shuffles your deck, so to speak, and forces you to hit the reset button on everything from priorities, to expectations, even to your sense of self. It's sobering to discover how little control you actually have."

"Exactly," she says softly, her eyes slowly drifting my way, as if seeing me for the first time.

There's a moment of recognition—an almost tangible

connection—when I look in her blue eyes and find her pain laid open.

"Who did you lose?" I whisper, and immediately regret it when I see those eyes well up.

"My son. My world," she says, breaking my heart with those softly uttered words.

Almost without conscious guidance, my hand reaches out and grabs hold of hers. "The first time I saw you," I confirm what I already know.

She nods and takes a deep breath. "Jamie was riding his bike along the sidewalk." She shakes her head like she still can't believe it, and her voice is almost monotone. She doesn't pull back her hand, though, it's like she grips my fingers tighter. "He'd done so many times before. His dad asked him to meet for lunch. It was just after noon on a Tuesday. They said the car just plowed onto the sidewalk. Who gets drunk in the middle of a workday?" She seems genuinely puzzled.

Something she said is nagging at me. "You said Tuesday?"

"Tuesday March twenty-seventh."

"But it was December when I—"

"I know. Jamie survived the crash. He had a severe concussion, and was paralyzed from his chest down, but he survived for another nine months. I'd just dropped him off with his physical therapist at Tufts and went to grab coffee when he collapsed during his daily exercise regimen. It was an aneurism. He was on life support for a week before he…"

"Jesus, Mika," I groan as I get to my feet and pull her up at the same time. Closing the distance and folding her in my arms happens without thinking. "I'm so sorry."

"Not wasting any time, are ya?" Daniel's taunt sounds behind me, and I've never before felt a stronger urge to plow my fist in my friend's face. Instead I keep my back turned and Mika shielded from the asshole.

"Shut up, you idiot," I hear Melissa hiss as their lowered voices disappear around the side of the cottage.

"There's more," Mika's voice is muffled in my shirt and I loosen my arms. Immediately she takes a step back. She looks wrecked, and I feel guilty for having brought this on.

"Not tonight. You're exhausted."

"But I need you to know that—"

My fingers press against her lips. "If you still want to, you can tell me another day. I'm not going anywhere. Get some rest."

I'm not sure if it's the vulnerable look in her blue eyes or the temptation of her soft lips under the pads of my fingers, but I can't seem to stop myself from leaning down and pressing a gentle kiss on her mouth.

Chapter Six

Mika

"ARE YOU SETTLING IN OKAY?"

This morning is the first chance I get to catch up with Sam. Saturday and Sunday had been crazy busy, both during lunch and at dinner.

I saw the truck come in Saturday morning, off-loading what I hoped was the dishwasher, while I was sipping coffee out front. I thought I was off the hook when Mandy showed up knocking on my door at noon. Trish, the woman who'd seemed a little distant the night before had apparently come down with something and—according to a brutally honest Mandy—I was conveniently close. That started my crash course as a server.

I never knew how exhausting waiting tables was. By the time the last customer cleared the restaurant last night, I vowed never to tip less than twenty percent again.

Instead of sitting outside, I'm holed up in the cottage this morning, covered in a blanket I pulled off the bed. It's miserable and chilly outside after a weekend of balmy temperatures.

"Better than I thought," I admit. "After this weekend, I almost feel like a local."

"Why? What did you do on the weekend?"

"Worked my ass off." I chuckle. It's true; I can still feel the burn in my legs and arms from being on my feet, carrying heavy trays.

"Worked? How? Where?"

"At the restaurant. Friday night I washed dishes and the rest of the weekend I served."

"You?" I can hear the disbelief in her voice.

I don't blame her, I can't really believe it myself, least of all how much I enjoyed it. I'd been nervous at first, not just that I might drop someone's lunch or dinner in their laps, but that I'd be recognized. The thing I never realized about waiting tables is that people don't really see you. Oh, they look at you, talk to you, even smile, but they don't really see the person standing in front of them.

Last night there'd been a table with two couples, and I'd caught one of the men staring at me. It was clear he was trying to place me after I'd taken their order. When I brought out their food, he snapped his fingers. "Didn't you used to work at the Bullpen? By Fenway Park?" I'd just smiled, nodded and told him it'd been quite some time since I'd been near that place. It's the truth, and the man seemed to take it as confirmation, which suited me just fine.

"Yes, Sam. Me."

"Wait. You mean his restaurant? You talked to him?"

I stay quiet, thinking about how close I came to spilling all the beans Friday night. I was tired and emotional, and almost told him everything, but he'd stopped me. Told me it could wait, except there hasn't been a chance since. Besides,

I'm not even sure I could bring up the courage. That night my defenses were down, but they're firmly back in place now.

No matter how attracted I am to him, or how unexpectedly safe I felt when he held me, there's no way I can allow myself to go there.

"Mika?"

"I did talk to him some. I...I told him about Jamie, but I didn't tell him everything."

"Mika..." Her tone is admonishing.

"I know, okay? I know...it's just...I like it here. I feel connected, and it's not just about the girl. It's him too. I don't want to have to leave, and if I tell him, I may have to."

"I get that, I do, but I'm afraid the longer you postpone the person who'll really be hurt is y—"

"I know," I quickly interrupt. "I just need a little more time, that's all."

There's a pregnant pause before she drops it and changes the topic. "By the way, I talked to Steve. He says it didn't even occur to him. Typical guy, he knows your story, he knows his friend's story, and still he wasn't able to put two and two together until I connected the dots for him."

"It's not his fault, Sam."

"Oh, I know, but he's my brother, so if it gives me something to lord over his head for a while, I'm gonna use it." I hear the grin in her voice and I'm chuckling myself. Sam adores her brother and vice versa, but they sure love to give each other a hard time. It's something I've always envied, that kind of relaxed relationship. "By the way," she continues. "He says he can try to find you another rental. Of course, he also mentioned you're welcome to stay at his place, but we'll ignore that. He's a dog."

"Yes, let's ignore," I agree with her. "And I have his number if I find myself in need of new digs."

We don't talk long after that, just a quick check on how her husband, Dennis, and their two girls are doing, before we say our goodbyes.

I get up off the couch to grab myself another coffee, when I notice the bowl of sea glass sitting on the counter. I let my fingers drag over the smoothly rounded pieces and realize I haven't thanked Jude for these yet. It had been more than just a nice gesture, something that was confirmed when he gave me that barely-there kiss. I may not be the brightest or most experienced person when it comes to the romance department, but I'm willing to wager Jude is interested in me too.

It's not what brought me here. I wasn't exactly looking for anything more than connecting with myself again. Still, the unexpected draw is there, and I can't help consider all the complexities it calls up.

As I pour my coffee, I notice sunlight is trying to break through outside. I'd resigned myself to an indoor day of reading, maybe catching a movie or something on the small TV, but it looks like I might still be able to do a little beach-combing.

Nothing like a cool sea breeze to clear the mind.

Jude

"WE HAVE A PROBLEM."

I look up to find Mandy standing in the doorway to my office.

"What now?"

She walks in and takes a seat on one of the visitor chairs, looking serious.

"I just got a call from Trish's husband. Apparently Trish was brought to Mass General on Sunday. She had a stroke."

"You're kidding me. She's my age. How is she?"

I'm shocked. Trish has worked here for close to ten years. I can count the times she's been off sick on one hand. She's as tough and strong as they come.

"Forty-eight, actually, and she's stable. Fred says the doctors are still running tests, but at this point her entire left side is paralyzed."

"Shit. Is there anything we can do? Anything Fred needs?"

"I offered. He said he'd call if he needs something, but he's got their daughter flying in from California this afternoon."

"Visitors?"

Mandy shakes her head. "She's in ICU, so just family for now."

"Fair enough. Let Fred know we can keep an eye on their house while they're in Boston, and to let us know when she's allowed visitors. Jesus, that's scary."

"I know and I will. Seems almost disrespectful at this point but we need to look at the summer schedule. Trish and Penny are our full-timers. I can try and fill Trish's shifts with the part-time roster, but most of them are students, and you know as well as I do, we need someone reliable. Someone we can count on to be here when they're supposed to be."

"It's not easy to find full-time staff during the season. Remember it took us forever to find Penny?"

"I don't think we'd have to look that far."

I squint my eyes and study her expression. She's already got a plan and I bet I know what it is. "You're talking about Mika."

She confirms it when she shrugs. "She's mature, she did fine this weekend on very short notice, and she's right here."

"Maybe so, but I'm pretty sure she didn't come here to wait fucking tables all summer."

"Only one way to find out, Boss. She's home now, I can go find out." She pushes out of her chair and makes for the door when I stop her.

"I'll do it."

"Suit yourself," she says, with a knowing little smile, before she disappears down the hallway.

Mandy will just manipulate her into saying yes, but I want to make sure Mika gets to make up her own mind.

With Kelty in my care, my hands are tied; otherwise, I could take over at least part of Trish's schedule myself. The only reason I was able to jump in this past weekend was because my daughter was at Cassie and Mark's place.

My phone rings just as I'm about to head over to the cottage. It's my dad calling.

"Hey, Dad. How are things?"

The last two years, since my mother passed away, my father's had a really hard time. At seventy-two, he's still in pretty good shape physically, and prior to Mom's death he was still very interested in the world around him, but since then he's been slipping.

My brother, Ethan, who lives with his family just north of Boston, keeps an eye on him. I call as much as I can, or pop by when I'm in town, but we can't make up for Mom's absence.

"I'm a'ight. How's that granddaughtah of mine?" My dad, whose Boston accent only seems to get thicker as he ages, adores Kelty. He loves all his grandchildren—Ethan has two teenage boys—but I guess Kelty is as much his 'princess' as she is mine.

"Doing good, Dad. She's keeping up with her school-work, but this is the last week before summer vacation sets in and she can't wait to be off the hook."

"I bet." Dad's raspy chuckle is good to hear.

"Why don't you come down?" I suggest, having a light bulb moment. "Drive down, pack enough so you can spend the summer with us? House is big enough, Dad."

"Ah, I don't know…"

"Think about it, I'd love for you to come, and I know Kelty would be over the moon. Truth is, Dad, I could use your help. I'm in a bit of a bind."

It's quiet on the other side for a moment while I wait for him to bite. "A bind?" he finally echoes. "What aw ya talking about?"

"Remember Trish? She had a stroke yesterday."

"Too young," he rumbles.

"You're not kidding. She appears to be stable, but no matter what, this isn't something you just bounce back from. Which leaves me short my best server. I can jump in, but there isn't a lot I can do with Kelty here. I'm not sure what your plans are for the summer, but…" I let my words trail off. I know damn well he's got nothing planned, but I want him to think about it.

"You need my help."

"Shit, Dad, I sure could use it. Only a few people I feel comfortable leaving Kelty with, ya know."

Again he makes me wait. He hasn't really been out of the house much in the past two years, and I know this won't be easy for him, but it may well be just what he needs.

"A'ight. Guess I could come for a while."

I try to keep the grin that's on my face from my voice. "Sooner the better, Dad. I appreciate it, it's a load off my shoulders."

Mandy isn't the only one good at manipulating people.

I'm glad when he offers to be here before the weekend. Maybe this will be a solution that benefits us all in the end.

Knowing I'll be able to shoulder part of the load, I feel better about approaching Mika for help. One down, one to go.

"Keep an eye on Kelty? I'll be right back," I call out to Mandy, who's behind the bar, on my way out.

Thankfully the sun is breaking through the thick deck of clouds we woke up to. Walking up to the cottage, I just catch Mika stepping out the door with a book and a mug in her hand.

It's a good thing the weekend was busy. I let my guard down Friday night when I kissed her. Feeling her soft lips under mine sent my attraction to stratospheric heights, terrifying the shit out of me. I can't recall ever feeling this strong, almost instinctual, draw to a woman.

It would be easy to forget she's just going to be here for the summer, especially now that she's working alongside me in the restaurant. I know it's probably smarter to keep a bit of distance, but I can't deny even just the sight of her does something to me.

"Morning," I call out.

"Hey," she returns with a cautious smile. I imagine she probably remembers last time we were on her porch. Or maybe I'm just hoping she does.

"Sorry to barge in. I have something to ask you."

I tell her about Trish—she appears as shocked as I was—about my dad coming out to help, before I ask if she'd be at all interested in more hours. She seems to hesitate before she answers.

"You mean take over all her shifts?"

"Even just a few a week would help, I can take care of the rest. But no pressure at all—I know you didn't really come here to work, and I don't know what your plans are—I just wanted to see if you'd be interested before I start hiring outside help."

Another pause.

"I don't really have set plans for the summer. I'd just like to do a bit of exploring. Bring my camera." She looks over at the restaurant and the water beyond, where I just notice the heron swooping in for a meal.

"Tips are good," I find myself encouraging her. "And meals are included." I catch myself, realizing how stupid I sound. I imagine she's not suffering as a sports journalist. "Not that it's necessarily a concern for you," I add, only shoving my foot in farther, but she surprises me.

"Actually, my plan was to get a job anyway." She grins half-heartedly. "It's amazing how much your financial situation can change in the span of a year."

Again I get the sense there is more to her story than what she's told me so far, but I keep from saying anything and just nod.

"When would I start?" she asks, and I have to bite my lip.

"My dad won't be here to look after Kelty until Thursday at the earliest, so how does five today sound?" I wince even as I'm asking, but she just smiles. This time without holding back, and it's stunning.

"I'll be there."

I don't let my own smile break through until I turn back to the restaurant.

Chapter Seven

Mika

YESTERDAY MORNING, Kelty joined me on the porch to watch for her heron.

Jude had lifted a few fingers acknowledging me, but continued on to the restaurant, carrying the little girl's pink Hello Kitty backpack in his other hand. I couldn't help grin.

She stayed until her dad called her over, mostly chatting about missing her school friends, her excitement about getting a new brother or sister, and how much she hates broccoli. I had to laugh at that, especially since it prompted a brief discussion on the merits of vegetables, with me arguing for and Kelty arguing against. It left us both smiling.

She's here again today, sitting on my step when I walk out with my coffee. My heart does a little leap at the sight of her almost white-blonde hair.

"Hey, missy. You're early today."

She tilts her head back and aims those crystal blue eyes my way. "We're leaving soon," she shares.

I sit beside her on the step. "Where are you off to today?" She told me about the day trips her father has taken her on as part of her homeschooling. It only makes the man more attractive.

There's something so sexy about a good father. I never knew one, and sadly Emmett wasn't exactly a good one for Jamie. It's definitely a turn-on.

"Dad's taking me whale watching," she says with a big smile. "I've wanted to go for…like…ever!" I chuckle at her theatrics. "But Dad said we could go today to celebrate summer."

"That's awesome. It's on my list of things to do this summer. I've never been, which is kinda weird, when you think about it."

"Why is it weird?"

"Because I've lived in and around Boston my whole life, and I know for a fact, there are whaling tours from Boston as well. I just never went on one."

"Maybe you were too busy?"

I smile at the earnest expression on her face. From the mouths of babes. "Maybe," I echo.

We both turn to the water to see if the heron's made his appearance.

I'm not sure why he strikes me as a *he*. It's not like I'm able to tell the difference, I wouldn't know where to start. Perhaps it's the self-assured, almost arrogant, way he claims his territory. Flying in with big swoops of his wings before stalking to his favorite hunting spot on those deceptively strong legs. Sure and unwavering, without a single hesitation. I imagine if it were a female, she would be more aware of her surroundings. Maybe more surreptitious in her approach: making sure not to draw too much attention to herself.

Or maybe I'm just projecting.

It's not that I don't think women can't be self-assured, or strong and unwavering. Hell, for years I've held my own in a male-dominated industry, but it wasn't easy to get there, nor was it easy to stay. I've had to prove myself over and over again. Show I could adjust and adapt to the good-ole-boy ways that are still so prevalent. Blend in and don't stand out too much.

It's one of the reasons I don't think I want to return to my career. I'm tired of meeting other people's expectations before my own.

I'm lost in thought when Kelty suddenly jumps up.

"There's Dad."

I look up to see his long legs close the distance, and I automatically get on my feet as well.

"You know, you should come," Kelty suddenly suggests, turning to face me.

"Come?" I ask, but it falls to deaf ears because the girl is already skipping to her dad, chattering in her girly voice.

"She can, can't she? Mika wants to see the whales anyway, and since we're going I think she should come. It's way more fun coming with us than going alone, right, Dad?"

"Honey, that's really sweet of you to ask, but…" I start to decline, hoping to save Jude the uncomfortable task of telling her no in front of me.

Except, her father's smile doesn't appear at all uncomfortable. "That's a great idea, actually. That is…" He turns his dark eyes on me and I can see the laugh lines fanning out from his eyes, proving he likes to smile and does it often. Another check mark on the pro side. "…if Mika can be ready in like…" He quickly checks his watch. "…five minutes tops, or we'll miss the boat."

"I'm supposed to start at four," I tell him.

"We'll be back here at three at the latest."

Wisdom tells me to say no, but fuck, I want to go. I want to go with *them*.

A hint of doubt starts to surface, but I force it into submission.

"Five minutes," I promise with a grin wide enough to split my face, as I rush inside to get ready.

I hear Kelty's excited whoop behind me.

I don't bother changing—my jeans and shirt will do just fine—but I do grab a hoodie and shove my feet in my red Chucks instead of my flip-flops, before snagging my camera and purse.

Apparently the wide grin is still on my face when I burst out of the door again, because it's immediately met with two matching ones that make me stop in my tracks.

Father and daughter: one dark, one fair, with smiles equally dazzling.

Good God, they make me feel alive.

Jude

"Is that them, Daddy?"

I look where Kelty is pointing. "Those are dolphins, Princess. They like swimming alongside the boat. We probably won't see anything until we round that lighthouse there." I indicate the Long Point Light Station.

"Did you see the dolphins?" she asks Mika, who comes down from the top deck where she was taking a few shots.

"I did. Got some pictures too. Wanna see?" She sits down on the narrow metal bench and Kelty slides in beside her right away, her eyes already focused on the small digital screen.

The drive here was filled with Kelty chattering from the back seat, and occasional furtive glances to my right. A few times I caught Mika's eyes checking me out. This woman makes me act like a fucking teenager.

It's crazy, I barely know her and already she feels familiar.

The only snag we had was when I parked the Traverse and told Kelty to put her mask on. It's just precautionary, but she's still on the high dose of immunosuppressants and the last thing she needs is to catch something. That's why whenever we go out, she wears her mask and I carry hand sanitizer with me. She knows why it's necessary, but she still doesn't like it.

Her eyes shot to Mika and her little chin lifted stubbornly. Without knowing why, Mika seemed to clue in quickly it was important, and asked if I happened to have any spares. I pointed to the glove box. She pulled one out, and without saying a word, covered her mouth and nose with it before getting out of the car. I got out as well and waited for my daughter. She eventually came out wearing hers.

No words were exchanged until we were in line to board the tour boat.

"You can take it off now," Kelty told Mika, who pulled the mask away from her face.

"I'm perfectly fine keeping it on if it makes it easier for you."

"It's okay, I'm used to it."

"Well, if you're sure…" Mika quickly got rid of her mask and tucked it in her pocket.

Now they're sitting side by side, two blonde heads bent over the digital camera. A casual observer might think they're related.

"Looks like we may have found a pod." A voice comes

over the sound system. *"Keep your eyes port-side—that's the left—just up ahead."*

People immediately flock to this side of the boat, and there's barely any standing room.

"Go stand by your dad," I hear Mika telling Kelty, who sneaks between me and the railing. In the distance we see the spray from a blowhole.

"Over there, I saw it." My girl grins up at me.

"I saw it too." I turn to Mika and gesture her over.

"It's okay. I'll get my chance."

"Excuse me," I tell the guy standing behind me. I reach around him, grab Mika's hand, and pull her toward me, tucking her between my daughter and me. "Now we can all see," I say, my lips by her ear, bracing my hands on the railing on either side of them.

Suddenly about twenty feet from the boat a spray shoots up, and the back of a whale curves out of the water. Two seconds later another humpback pops up, right beside it. Mika's hand curls around my wrist and I feel her body tense against mine.

"There's one on the other side too," someone calls out, and half the crowd scurries to the starboard railing, leaving us with more room.

"Can we go?" Kelty asks.

"Stay here, Princess. Keep your eyes to the front of the boat." To Mika, I say, "Get your camera ready." Reluctantly I lift my hand from the railing so she can find a better spot, while I step closer to my daughter.

"Daddy, look at the tail!"

I quickly shift my attention from watching Mika's shapely ass move in those formfitting jeans, back to the ocean. A large tail lifts out of the water, spraying droplets, and my daughter is jumping up and down in front of me.

For almost half an hour the pod of whales hangs around the boat, giving us a great show, before they move on and the boat turns back to the harbor.

Kelty is quiet and a little pale, so we sit down and I encourage her to put her head on my leg. When Mika finds us, she looks at my daughter with concern clear on her face.

"Is she okay?" she whispers, taking a seat beside me.

"Tired," I explain, and then I figure I might as well fill her in on all of it. "Kelty was diagnosed with acute cardiomyopathy, March of last year. She had a heart transplant in December." I watch as the blood drains from Mika's face. "She's fine now," I reassure her, putting a hand on her knee. "She just still burns through her energy quickly, which is why I push the afternoon naps." Mika's eyes say focused on Kelty's closed eyes, but she nods in understanding. "The mask is because of her medication."

"Immunosuppressants," she mumbles.

"Yeah. That's why she's homeschooled. At least these past months. We'll reassess in July and see if maybe she can go back to school after the summer break."

"That's good. So she's doing okay? Her new heart?" Her eyes, still worried, now focus on me.

"Yeah. Her cardiologist is happy. She had one brief rejection episode when she was still in the hospital but nothing since. Knock on wood."

"Good." She nods her head and then repeats, "That's good."

She stays quiet, sitting beside me and seemingly unaware of my hand still resting on her knee, until the boat pulls alongside the dock.

"Should we wake her up?"

"You take my truck keys, I'll carry her," I suggest.

She leads the way onto the dock and I follow her to the parking lot, my sleep-heavy daughter in my arms.

"Wait," Mika says when we get to the truck and quickly opens the back door, making room so I can lay my girl on the back seat.

"I'd hoped to take you for lunch," I admit, as we drive through Provincetown, back to the main road.

"That's okay."

"Rain check?" I ask, reaching over to take her hand. For a minute it feels like she might pull it back, but then she slips her slender fingers between mine.

"Yeah."

We don't talk much during the half hour it takes us to get home, but her hand never leaves mine. When I pull into my driveway, the dashboard clock shows one thirty.

"Would you mind opening my front door?" I ask, handing her my key chain again.

I notice her looking around my living room when we walk in. I put Kelty, who's still out for the count, on the couch. Mika is ready with the throw from the armrest, draping it carefully over my daughter before turning to me, a little smile on her face.

"I should get home."

"I'll walk you," I announce.

"It's broad daylight, Jude. I think I should be able to find it," she quips, lifting a single eyebrow.

"Humor me."

She rolls her eyes, but doesn't say anything more when I follow her out the door.

"Thank you," she says stopping at the top of her steps. "That was a mind-blowing experience, and I can't believe I've lived so close all my life and never made it out before."

"I didn't either for the longest time. Not until I moved out here."

I take another step closer, not quite ready to say goodbye.

"Well, thanks for inviting me."

She turns to the door and I close the distance stopping right behind her. "Ask me in."

"Sorry?" She swings her head around, a bit confused.

"Ask me in, Mika."

Her eyes scan my face for a long moment before she nods and opens the door, stepping aside to let me in. I stand facing her until she closes the door behind her, then I move in.

Her sharp inhale is sexy as hell as I brace my hands against the door, on either side of her head. The next sound from her is a deep groan when I lean in, cover her mouth with mine, and slip my tongue between her slightly parted lips. Her taste, rich and heady, floods my senses and instantly makes me crave more.

I force my hands to stay where they are, otherwise I might strip her right where she stands. The only thing connecting us is our lips; it's the most intimate kiss I've ever shared.

Chapter Eight

Mika

"DID YOU HAVE A GOOD TIME?"

I look up to find Mandy grinning at me. Immediately my mind goes to the soul-scorching kiss Jude planted on me just a few hours ago.

A good time would be an understatement; my head is still spinning with the impact of his mouth on mine. Unlike the previous peck he planted on me—which already carried a punch—this kiss had woken up parts of me that had been dormant for a very long time. Heck, it had shaken me so badly that even long after he abruptly ended the kiss and stalked out the door, I hadn't been able to draw a proper breath.

"Huh?"

Humor flashes in Mandy's eyes at my unintelligible response. "Whale watching, did you enjoy it?"

Realization floods me and with it a healthy blush at where my mind had automatically gone. "Yes. It was unbelievable,"

I quickly answer. "You should see some of the pictures. The moment I have a chance I'm going to edit them; I'll show you."

"Jude mentioned you like photography," she shares, and I wonder when he would've told her that. Or why. "Said you were good. He's been looking at new decor for the restaurant for a while." I look around at the collection of prints and watercolors on the walls. Pretty images of the cove, some of the Cape's lighthouses, and a large canvas some artist must've done right here on his property. It depicts the restaurant, the main house, and my cottage against the water. Pretty enough, but a bit of a rambling assortment without much of a collective input. "He said he might approach you about it. I was just wondering if he mentioned anything. Since I saw you come back with your camera," she adds.

If she saw me come back, the likelihood is she would've seen Jude go into my cottage as well.

Again, the heat of a blush warms my cheeks. "He didn't. Mention anything, I mean. Besides, the photography, it's just a hobby. Something I enjoy doing. Mostly for myself."

Mandy wipes a rag over the bar, but keeps a scrutinizing glance aimed at me. "There's a place called The Cape PhotoArt & Framing, just south of the rotary. They specialize in photo printing. You should go check them out."

I'd driven by the place a few times and had made a mental note to stop in one day. Most of my pictures—save a few I'd printed out and hung up in my old bedroom—never made it beyond the digital format. Just pretty snaps for me to browse through every so often. I like playing with filters and overlays—creating different moods and atmospheres and giving my shots a more artistic flair—but those creations have never made it off my laptop. It's always just been something to do.

"I guess I could check it out someday," I concede, down-playing the kernel of excitement growing in my gut.

"Up to you," Mandy says with a nonchalant shrug of her shoulders, as if she didn't just light a fire in my belly.

Lucky for me the restaurant is not crazy busy tonight, because half the time I'm walking around mentally cataloguing my photographs into a portfolio. Yet, I only get one drink order wrong.

It's not until I roll into bed a little after eleven that I allow myself to think about the kiss again. He never even touched my body, and yet every inch of my skin tingles at the memory.

Electric. Combustive. One stroke of his hand would have incinerated me.

The effect he has on me is dangerous, but the fire I'm playing with has a far more devastating potential.

It wrecked me when he started talking about Kelty's condition. I almost told him to stop, but he gifted me with that trust, and coming clean in that moment—telling him I already knew—would have thrown that gift back in his face. I realize the hole I'm digging myself only gets deeper, but I can't seem to help myself.

This wonderful man and his precious daughter are addictive.

"Is it hard to learn?"

Kelty was back on my steps this morning when I came out with my coffee. She already had breakfast, she informed me, and then asked if she could see yesterday's pictures.

I must've snapped a few hundred at least. It takes us quite a while to scroll through, and Kelty points at her favorites.

I'm actually quite surprised myself at how well some of these turned out. It's much different to shoot something inanimate that you can adjust your settings for to get the best results. Shooting something that moves unpredictably is much harder. You don't have time to perfect exposure or lighting or any of those things, it's more of a Hail Mary, hoping you caught the action at exactly the right moment.

Thank God for image bursts that allow me to rapid shoot an entire sequence with one press of the button. The result is a few great shots of the whale rising out of the water with every drop of the spray he created clearly defined.

"It's not really hard to do. All it takes is holding the camera steady and pushing a button," I explain. "The hardest part, I think, is finding interesting things to take pictures of, and have the pictures be exactly what it looked like with the naked eye. That's the real tricky part."

She's quiet for a moment, looking like she's thinking hard. "You know," she starts, and I almost chuckle at her tone combined with that serious face. "I think I could find things to take pictures of."

"I bet you could," I encourage her, tempted to give her the smaller camera tucked in my camera bag to experiment with.

It had been a present for Jamie's tenth birthday. It was a pretty generic point and click camera, with a fully automatic setting, but it also gave him the option of adjusting settings manually to experiment. Jamie used to love the 'photo-adventures' we'd sometimes go on whenever I had some time off. It had given us something in common at a time in his life when I could feel him growing up and away from me. In hindsight, I should've made an effort to create more of those memories. Just one of many regrets.

The thought of taking Kelty under my wing—teaching her about lighting and composition—is an enticing prospect.

She's not my child, though, I should definitely check with her father before I make any promises.

God forbid I overstep any more boundaries than I already am.

Jude

"Grampa!"

Kelty shoots by me out the door, the moment I open it to my dad lumbering up the steps.

It's difficult noticing him look older every time I see him. He even moves like an old man now.

"Hey, Peanut." His deep rumble is still familiar, though. An immediate comfort.

I watch as my father folds Kelty in his arms, pressing his cheek to the top of her head. It invokes memories of me pressing my ear to his chest, feeling his deep voice vibrating against me as he talked. I remember wishing I'd have a reverberating voice like his when I grew up, but instead I ended up with a smoker's rasp, when I've never smoked a day in my life.

"Son." His eyes meet mine as he lets his granddaughter go and I go out to meet him.

"Glad you're here, Dad." I give him a hug and get a few bone-crushing slaps to my back.

He was already working on the docks when he met my mom almost fifty years ago. A gruff man, with very little in the way of social skills, who fell head over heels for the pretty librarian. They were polar opposites; everything about my mom was soft and refined, in contrast with all my dad's rough edges. Still, they loved each other and over the years, Mom managed to smooth out some of his gruffness. Even taught him how to show affection to his sons, which wasn't always easy for him. It's not the way he was raised for sure. He did well by us, though, and my brother and I learned to take the bruises with the love.

"Me too, boy. She's looking better."

"Getting better too, Dad."

I see him swallow hard before nodding. "That's good."

Kelty's diagnosis had almost done him in. Following so shortly to Mom dying, the initial news his granddaughter might not have long to live wreaked havoc, and there were times I'd been afraid of losing him too.

"Princess, grab Grampa a coffee, will you? He could probably use one. Dad, give me your keys and I'll fetch your stuff."

I round the front of the house when I spot Mika walking over to the restaurant. She sees me too and shoots me a hesitant smile. I lift my chin.

It's not a surprise when she keeps walking, after losing my mind kissing her yesterday, I just about ran out of the cottage. She must think I'm certifiable.

The truth is, she scares me. Or rather, the feelings she evokes scare me. It's pretty intense and for a moment when my mouth held her captive, with her back against the door, I forgot everything else.

I can't afford to forget everything else.

My daughter depends on me. So do her mother and Mark. This is not the right time for me to lose my head, among other things.

I'd underestimated the effect Mika has on me, and now that I've felt its full potential, I'm second-guessing the wisdom of pursuing anything. What if I lose myself in her and she packs her bags at the end of her stay? Or what if something goes wrong in the meantime? My daughter is already more than halfway in love with her, and it wouldn't take much for me to tumble down that same rabbit hole. Then there's her working at the restaurant as well.

This woman rolled in like a tsunami, flooding every aspect of my life. And she's not even doing it on purpose.

Fuck, I've told a few women I loved them—and meant it at the time—but I've never had the urge to make a life-long commitment, let alone based on a single kiss. Still, it wouldn't have been hard to convince me yesterday, and that scared the crap out of me.

I'm glad to see Dad brought more than just one suitcase. Having him here might prove to be just the distraction I need.

"Mr. Parks!"

Mandy comes around the bar and greets Dad like a long-lost favorite uncle. A role he's always enjoyed when he visited before. Of course Mandy has a way of making everyone feel welcome.

Dad can't hide his pleased little smile. Nothing like a pretty young woman making a fuss to have the old geezer spark with some life.

"Ah ya done with that man of yaws yet?" he asks, his eyes twinkling. "Nevah gonna give me a chance, aw ya?"

"Truth is," Mandy says, familiar with Dad's game. "I don't think I could handle a man like you, Mr. Parks."

"Bullocks. And quit calling me *mistah*, making me feel old. It's Jim."

"Fair enough, *Jim*," she emphasizes with a grin. "Have a

seat and I'll bring you some drinks. You still like that Trillium brew your son keeps stocked for you?"

"Don't mind if I do."

Kelty is already seated at her favorite table. It's in the corner where she can see out on the cove, as well as to the side where her heron often appears for breakfast or dinner. That is, until the patio opens, when she prefers to sit outside if there's room.

"Good evening." The formal greeting sounds a little awkward from Mika's mouth as she walks up to the table.

"Hi, Mika, guess what? My granddad's here."

She doesn't hold anything back when she smiles at my daughter and I feel that too.

"That's great, honey," she says, turning the smile on my dad, who looks at her through slitted eyes.

"Who's this?" is the first thing out of his mouth.

"Dad, this is Mika, she's filling in while Trish is recovering in the hospital."

His eyes dart to me. "How's Trish doin'?"

"Spoke to her husband this morning. Things seem to be looking a bit better. The doctors say since she's still young, her chances of a full recovery are good, but it's gonna take time."

He grunts before he looks back at Mika. "You don't look like a waitress to me," he says, and I groan internally when I see her wince.

"Dad," I try, but Kelty, in all her innocence, jumps in.

"She's a photographer, Grampa."

"A photographah?" He doesn't look convinced, scrutinizing the poor woman, who is starting to fiddle with her notepad.

"Yeah," Kelty says undeterred. "She takes pictures of my

heron, and yesterday she came with us whale watching and she took pictures of them too. I want to learn photography."

That draws the old man's attention, and mine too.

"Ya do?"

"Yeah, it's so cool. You first have to find things that are interesting, and then the light has to be right, and the comp...compos..."

"Composition," Mika softly fills in.

"That a fact?" Once again his squinting eyes take her in.

"I'll just give you a minute and grab your drinks," she quickly mutters before walking away from the fire. I don't blame her.

"Dad..." My tone is level, but I know he can hear the threat.

"What? She's an interesting package."

"Don't call her that."

"Dunno what else to call her. One day I'm watching her interview Belichick on the tube, the next she's waiting tables in yaw restaurant, and now my granddaughter tells me she's a photographah. I'd say that makes her an interesting package."

Of course my dad would recognize her. I should've known; he's intimately acquainted with every damn sports-caster on the Eastern Seaboard.

"Just don't harass her, Dad," I plead, to which he harrumphs loudly.

Chapter Nine

Mika

"Mika?"

I'm about to open my car door when I hear Jude's voice.

I haven't actually spoken to him, other than during work hours, since I mustered up the courage to approach him about the camera Friday afternoon.

"Are you sure?" he'd asked in the relative quiet of his office. "That camera's gotta hold memories for you."

"It does," I confessed, "but I like the idea of someone else making good use of it better than it collecting dust somewhere."

He'd nodded and appeared to be deep in thought before responding.

"Let me think on it, okay?"

I can't say I wasn't disappointed, but the weekend was busy enough not to dwell on it too long. The first weekend of June apparently brings an influx of vacationers to the Cape, and although the restaurant had been busy during lunches, a lineup had started forming for dinner seating as well.

With the patio now open, Mandy had scheduled two extra pairs of hands, in addition to Penny and myself. Jude was around, but mostly jumped in behind the bar from time to time so Mandy could help on the tables.

He seemed evasive all weekend, and already conflicted myself, I figured he had regrets of his own and did my share of avoiding.

Hearing his voice out here has me square my shoulders before I turn around and watch him close the distance.

"Yes?"

"Do you have a minute or are you in a hurry?"

"I'm not rushed."

He suddenly seems at a loss for words as he runs his hand through his already unruly hair. "About last Wednesday," he starts, and I inadvertently brace myself against what's coming. I assumed he wanted to talk about Jamie's camera. I feel a bit blindsided so I carefully steel my features. He looks at me inquisitively before breathing out a deep sigh and rubbing his chin. "Look, you...*shit*...I've felt a draw...to you...since we first ran into each other at Tufts. I don't know why, or what, but when I saw you again in the lobby last month, it was still there. Then you turned out to be my tenant for the summer." He lowers his eyes as he raises his eyebrows and shakes his head. "Almost too good to be true. But it didn't stop there; my staff adopted you in very short order, as did my daughter. It only seemed to get better." He pauses again as his eyes find mine. "And then I kissed you—"

I quickly hold up my hand, afraid that if I listen any more, I'll burst out crying. This is it. I won't be able to stay now. I'm going to miss that little girl, and I haven't even had a chance to come clean. "I get it," I manage, reaching for my car door, but his hand intercepts mine.

"No. I don't think you do," he disagrees, holding firmly to my fingers. "Kissing you was…" He blows his breath through his lips. "Amazing? Mind-blowing, for sure. At least for me it was. Just talking about it makes me want to kiss you again." I startle at his confession. That's not what I expected to follow at all. "But see, the thing is, I know when I do it won't be so easy to take a step back. It's going fast. Not you," he quickly adds. "It's me. My daughter is my priority, first and foremost, and already she's attached to you. What if this…whatever's happening here…ends badly? You said you came here to find yourself, what if you get as lost in me as I could get in you? Where would that leave you? Where would that leave Kelty?"

I'm in shock. Mostly because he's voicing similar concerns to mine, with one major difference: I have knowledge that might change his entire perception of me.

"I hear you. And you're right, I probably could easily get lost in you. It wouldn't be fair; because there's a lot you don't know about me yet. A lot I haven't even wrapped my head around myself."

"Your son," he suggests and I nod.

"For one, yes. Just like Kelty is the main focus in your life, Jamie was that for me. My purpose. When that disappears, it changes the entire framework of your existence." His hand just squeezes mine and I'm grateful he doesn't give me platitudes. "My emotions are still raw," I forge on. "I feel things…almost too fast…and I can't tell how much of that is real. I'm just getting my feet wet, I can't quite trust myself yet."

Then he does something else unexpected and takes me into his arms. "We slow down. Take the pressure off and deal with whatever comes. If this pull between us is all it promises to be, a little downshift won't change where it will end up."

I only manage to nod, a little sad, but also a lot relieved. Mostly relieved, actually.

He sets me back a step, smiles, and presses his lips to my forehead. The gentle and caring gesture immediately brings tears to my eyes.

Fuck, I haven't had this since my mother died many years ago. I smile up at him, blinking against the tears and turn to my car when he starts walking back to the house.

"Oh, and, Mika?" he says, looking over his shoulder. "If you're still sure you want to do this, I think Kelty would love the camera. Her tenth birthday is coming up next week. She's been nagging me for one all weekend," he adds with a mischievous grin.

I'm still smiling myself as I make my way to Nauset Beach to look for sea glass and photo ops.

Jude

"More coffee, Dad?"

I ignore the inquiring glance my old man follows me with as I come back into the kitchen. I'm not sure what bug he has up his ass about Mika, but he's been pretty obvious about his disapproval of her. Fuck, he hasn't even given her a chance to do anything wrong.

"Saw ya out there with that woman," he grumbles, determined to get his word in.

"Jesus, Dad. What do you have against her?" I finally snap, my patience worn thin. I'm already questioning the wisdom of having him come. This is the kind of added stress I don't need.

"Ya hear things." He shrugs like he's done talking, but I'm not done. I quickly check to see that Kelty is still watching a show on TV before closing the kitchen door.

"What things, Dad? She's a good woman, who's been through enough. She doesn't need you making her life harder for no damn good reason."

"I see she's already got ya head turned," he grumbles. His head snaps up when my fist hits the counter.

"What is your problem, Dad?" I bark a little too loudly, and I keep my eye on the door to make sure Kelty doesn't barge in.

"Been all ovah the news in Boston, boy. Not an accident she's hidin' up heah. Trying to get out of the heat, I'm guessin'. Fought her ex-husband in cawt just so she could pull the plug on her boy. The husband tells it all ovah the papers. Ink weren't even wet on the cawt ordah and she had 'em shut off the machines. Man is devastated."

It's clear my father buys into this story, but he doesn't know I saw the woman walk down that hallway, her world destroyed. If any of it is true, she had a reason. There's not a doubt in my mind that boy was her life.

"Weren't you the one who taught me not to jump to conclusions?" I remind him. "That you shouldn't make judgments without all the necessary information? I distinctly remember you saying those things to me. I don't claim to know what the full story is—she told me her boy was on life support and then died—but Dad, it wrecked her." The flash of guilt on his face tells me I scored a point. "Don't go crucifying her based on half a story, because what I've seen and know of her, there isn't a malicious bone in Mika's body."

The temptation is substantial to log onto the internet and

dig up whatever Dad is talking about, but I don't. I trust my gut, and it tells me her ex-husband is a sniveling coward, dragging her name through the mud like that.

I'm sure there's lots I don't know yet—just as she doesn't really know much about my history—but I'd rather she tell me herself when she's ready.

DAD OPTED NOT to drive into Boston with us for Kelty's cardio checkup.

I'm not sure whether he's still pissed at me for reading him the riot act, whether he just didn't feel up to the drive, or he's just avoiding the hospital. He's never been a fan. I suspect it might be a combination of all of them. These trips may be getting a little tedious, but I'm always relieved when we leave with a thumbs-up on her health.

We're one visit away from her six-month mark, when they'll assess whether or not they can reduce her immunosuppressants slowly. Kelty is not a fan of the pills she has to take every day, but she understands how important they are.

It had killed to explain to our then eight-year-old daughter that she was very seriously ill. She didn't need us to spell out there was a chance she might not survive, she clued into it on her own, and that realization was the worst moment of my life, bar none. She's my girl, my princess, and those big blue eyes landed on me expecting her daddy to fix it. Fix her. Except for once there was absolutely nothing I could do for her.

Even now I can still feel that impotence. That lack of control.

Instead I drive her into the hospital twice a month. Watch as they draw her blood, when I know she hates the needles.

Test, probe, and prod her until she's so exhausted she can barely keep her head up and I often end up carrying her out to the parking lot.

I did so tonight, and I'd expected her to be asleep, but when I look in my rearview mirror, I catch her eyes on me from the back seat.

"Hey, Princess. I thought you'd still be asleep."

"Why were you fighting with Grampa this morning?"

Fuck. I knew I was too loud. Now I'm stuck in a dilemma, do I brush it off, or do I tell her the truth?

If Kelty was any other kid, I'd probably brush it off, but she's not. Sadly circumstances have made her wiser and more observant than she should be. Chances are she's noticed her grampa's attitude toward Mika and may be confused about the reasons as well.

Truth it is. At least a moderated version of it.

"Grampa hasn't been very nice to Mika, and I wanted to know why."

"Mika is nice," she volunteers.

"I agree. Now you know she used to be on TV, right? A sports reporter?" I take her nod as a yes. "Well, Grampa recognized her and he had heard some gossip about her that wasn't very nice."

"Gossip is never nice."

My eyes catch hers again in my mirror and I smile. "That's true. But it's a little more complicated because Grampa read it in the newspaper. Anyway, that's what we were arguing about. I know if Grampa just gives her a chance, he'll see for himself the gossip can't be true."

"I like Mika."

"Already mentioned that, Princess," I remind her, grinning as I watch her roll her eyes.

"I mean, you like her too, right?"

I can feel where this is going but am not sure how to avoid it without lying, so I keep it simple. "I like her."

"Right, and I know she likes you, because she always has this little smile when she looks at you. Plus," she quickly adds when she thinks I'll interrupt, "she has photos of you."

"Photos of me?"

"From the boat."

"She showed you?"

"Yeah. She has a few of me and you together as well. She wouldn't do that if she didn't like us, right?"

"I guess," I admit, before teasing, "unless they're really ugly photos. I don't think she really likes us much if she takes ugly pictures."

"They're nice, Daddy."

"Good to know, baby," I mumble.

Chapter Ten

Mika

ANOTHER BEAUTIFUL MORNING greets me when I pull open the door.

As does the unexpected guest sitting on my steps, a little taller and darker than my regular visitor.

I sit down beside him and follow his gaze over the water as the cove wakes up.

I haven't seen much of him this past week except at the restaurant. Other than a few meaningful glances, most interaction had been work-related and in the presence of others. So I'm a little surprised to find he sought me out this morning.

"My daughter tells me you took my pictures."

My eyes dart to his handsome profile.

"I did. Hers too."

He slowly turns his head to me. "Kelty has a theory. She says you can tell a person likes you when they take your picture, but I suggested it all depends on how that picture turns out."

I tilt my head. "Is this your convoluted way of telling me you want to see the pictures I took last week?"

He shrugs his shoulders and one corner of his lips tilt up in a grin, reminding me how tempting his mouth can be in close proximity. I force myself to look away.

"Wouldn't mind a coffee either," he mumbles under his breath and this time when I look back, he's full-on smiling.

I quickly get to my feet. "Very well, come on in. I have them all downloaded to my laptop, it's easier to see."

He follows me inside and I resist the urge to look at him when I hear the door close. Instead I busy myself with his coffee.

"Where's your daughter this morning, anyway?" I ask him as I pour fresh water into my Keurig.

"We had a late night watching a movie. She's sleeping in. Dad's driving her to Chatham when she wakes up. With her birthday tomorrow, and Cassie still confined to her bed, her mom wanted a chance to celebrate with her at their house. Mark should have her back here around noon. Kelty's a little disappointed there won't be a big party again, but it would just wipe her out. At least it's an improvement on last year when she missed out completely. Maybe for her next birthday we can make up for it."

"Poor kid," I commiserate.

"She'll get stronger. She's already improved a lot. The first weeks after the transplant she was weak as a newborn kitten. Even just going to the bathroom tired her out. She's come a long way."

"I'm glad," I share.

"Anyway, I was hoping you'd join us for burgers and cake tomorrow afternoon? At the restaurant. My daughter requested the patio. We'll aim for around three, before we have people showing up for dinner."

"Are you cooking?" I tease him. I've been told by more than one person, over the past couple of weeks, while Jude may be a top-notch restaurateur, he can't cook for shit. They tease him relentlessly.

He throws me a fake scowl. "Rest assured, Daniel will be doing the cooking."

"In that case, I'd love to. Are you okay with me giving her the camera then?" I ask. I'd planned to give it to her when she dropped by in the morning, but she'll be at her mom's.

"She'll be over the moon, and so will I. She's relentless when she has her eyes set on something."

I shove a mug under the spout and dig through my collection of coffee pods. "Dark roasted?"

"Please."

I press the button and turn around, leaning my elbows on the counter. "So other than Kelty's birthday, my stellar coffee, and the pictures, what brings you here today?"

"Am I that obvious?"

"Not really," I admit. "But I noticed you have this habit of rubbing your chin when you're trying to figure out what to say next, and you've been rubbing it since we came inside."

He immediately puts his hand down.

"Dad," he starts and I straighten a little. The older man has been in the restaurant daily, and although not as overtly hostile as the first few times, I could still feel him scrutinizing me from a distance. "I called him out on the way he behaved toward you last week." He notices the wince on my face. "Honestly, my dad is normally a pretty laid-back guy, which made his behavior out of character."

"He's been fine. Well," I catch myself, "better anyway. Do you know whether it's something I did?"

"God no. And I didn't really want to bring it up, but with my brother, his family, and few friends stopping by, I don't want you to be blindsided."

"By what?" I'm utterly confused.

"Do you know your ex has been talking to the media?"

I snort. It doesn't surprise me; he made our brief battle in court very public. Something the judge hadn't been very happy about because he'd clearly instructed—for the sake of privacy—details around the crux of the case be kept from the public. That actually suited Emmett just fine, since he was more interested in portraying me as a cold-hearted bitch anyway, which wasn't hard to do without providing full disclosure. It's one of the reasons I wanted out of Boston.

"I do. He's been doing this a while. I'm guessing your father got wind of it?"

He nods, looking down at the mug he has in his hand. "It's not exactly nice, the stuff your ex is saying."

I take in a deep breath. "Believe me, I know. I had to deal with it during the worst period of my life. He's always been very good at spouting so-called facts without context. He's angry and determined to take it out on me, and he won't stop until he's made it so no one will touch me. Nothing I can do to change it."

He stares at me for a long time, looking for something, an explanation maybe? Justification?

"You don't strike me as someone who'd so easily give up. Why don't you sue for defamation of character or something?"

I drop my head between my shoulders. It's a valid question, to which there is no satisfactory answer. Not now, not when he's gearing up for his daughter's birthday and has friends and family coming to celebrate. It wouldn't be fair to drop that on him today.

Besides, it's a catch-22 at this point; if I share it all with him now, I might clear my name, but the knowledge will still hurt him. Damned if I do, damned if I don't.

"I can't. If this was just about me, I would be fighting tooth and nail, but it isn't." I reach over the counter and grab his hand. "Do you trust me?"

It's a loaded question and I know it, but I'm asking anyway. I can see the struggle waging behind those brown eyes as he scans mine, and it kills to watch.

"I told my dad not to make judgments until we have all the information. I also told him I don't believe there is a malicious bone in your body. I stand by that."

Relief has me drop my forehead to our locked hands. "Thank you."

"But, Mika," he continues, "I feel like I'm flying blind here. I have so many questions."

"I know, and you'll have your answers, I promise, but first we celebrate your beautiful daughter's birthday."

It's selfish, but I want to see her celebrate her tenth birthday. I want to give her Jamie's camera, and I hope she'll make good use of it when I'm gone.

Then I plan to take that memory with me when I have to leave.

Jude

I watch Mika's reaction when we walk in.

Her smile for me is reserved, unlike the wide-open one she directs at Kelty.

'Happy birthday, honey," she calls out, opening her arms when my daughter immediately heads her way.

There isn't a hint of artifice in the way she hugs her, and I'm not the only one who notices.

"At least that seems to be genuine," my father grumbles behind me, and I press my lips together.

I never did end up seeing those pictures yesterday, but I did spend most of my time since then mulling over our conversation. It would've been easier if she'd just come out and claimed those stories about her were all lies, but she didn't do that. She did make it clear there was more to them than what her ex had been spreading.

Part of me wanted to shake it out of her, but when she implied she was protecting someone else, I backed off.

Through the windows, I'm surprised to see streamers and balloons decorating the patio, and judging from Kelty's excited squeal, she's spotted them too.

"Thank you," I mouth at Mandy, who's taking her turn congratulating my daughter, but she shakes her head, tilting it in Mika's direction. I walk up to the group and step to Mika's side, leaning in. "You didn't have to do that."

"A girl turns ten only once. She's double digits now, it's a big deal," she says under her breath, smiling as Kelty is being passed between the rest of my crew, getting hugs from everyone. Then her eyes turn to me. "I thought you said you had family and friends coming?"

"My brother, Ethan, and his wife, Libby, plus their two teenage boys should be here soon, and most of my friends are already here."

It's true, my circle was never that big, but it's gotten even smaller since my daughter first got sick. It's the people I work with on an everyday basis, who didn't shy away. Not that they really had a choice, Kelty's been a prominent feature in the restaurant since she was a baby. They'd had a front row seat on her life.

The only other person who stuck close was Steve, who I'm sure will show up at some point.

"Mika," my father says with a nod, when he joins our huddle.

"Congratulations on your granddaughter's birthday, Mr. Parks," she says with a tight smile. The old coot just grunts. Can you say passive aggressive? Dad prefers being called Jim and is forever correcting people who call him mister. I'm sure it hasn't escaped Mika he hasn't with her.

Fuck that, I'll do it for him.

"It's Jim, Mika. Dad doesn't care for formalities, do you, Dad?" I elbow him in the ribs.

"Jim it is," she says, her mouth still a little tense.

The stubborn old man doesn't say a thing, but when Mandy invites everyone out on the patio, he grabs my arm and holds me back. "That hurt," he says, looking pissed.

"Good," is all I have to say before I turn my back on him.

We've barely sat down when my brother and his family walk in. More hugs, and a brief moment of awkwardness when Kelty proudly introduces Mika to her cousins. The oldest, Ben, almost sixteen, seems to do a double take.

"Wait a minute, I've seen you on TV," he blurts out. "You were interviewing Brad Marchand." Before I can come to the rescue, Mika resolves the situation herself.

"A previous lifetime, kid," she says easily before she leans in and says in a low, conspiratory voice. "Nice guy, but did you know he's really short when he's not wearing skates?"

My nephew perks up. Good call, since Ben, at five foot nine, was outgrown by his younger brother two years ago and it's still a sore point, no matter how many times he's assured that guys can keep growing into their twenties.

I look over at Ethan, who seems to be observing the interaction as Mika manages to rope Ben into helping her get drinks for everyone. If my brother is aware of who she is, or the stories doing the rounds, he's not showing it. He's the levelheaded one of the bunch, much like Mom, whereas Dad and I may appear laid-back but tend to be more passionate.

When it's time for presents—after burgers but before cake—I'm surprised to see Mika coming outside with not just a smaller gift, I assume is the camera, but with a much larger one as well.

She waits until Kelty has unwrapped her last gift before she hands her the big one first. My suspicions are confirmed when the beautiful print is revealed. One of Mika's images of the white heron.

"Is that mine?" Kelty asks, her voice pitched even higher than normal.

"You bet it is, honey," Mika says, smiling at her.

"Great print," Ethan observes, as he takes in the image of the great white heron coming in for a landing, his wings spread wide and legs extended, barely clearing the water.

"Mika's a photographer. This is one of hers," I tell him, and even I can hear the pride in my voice.

"Actually…this isn't mine," she says and I turn to look at her. "It's Kelty's. She took it with my camera earlier this week."

My daughter's face is beaming with pride and a lump lodges in my throat as I try to smile at her. There is no way to express the feelings that overwhelm me.

I just stare at my little girl, surrounded by words of stunned surprise and praise.

"I guess everyone agrees when I said you had talent," I

hear Mika say and focus on her. "Which is why I think you're ready for this." She hands her the smaller package. "I should warn you, it's not new, but it belonged to someone who loved it as much as I hope you will."

I hear Kelty's gasp as she rips the paper off, but my eyes are locked with Mika's over my daughter's head. I know what this means to her, and I hope she understands it means a lot to me too.

"Christ, babe, you look smokin'!"

My head twists to the door, just in time to see my best friend, Steve, charging at Mika, lifting her straight up before swinging her around in his arms.

And she? She throws her head back and laughs, her arms wrapped around his neck.

What the ever-loving fuck?

Chapter Eleven

Jude

"YOU KNOW HER."

Steve turns his head when I walk into the men's room.

I'd managed to keep a polite front while Steve did the rounds, and wished Kelty a happy birthday.

I stayed quiet while we had cake, and while Mandy and Mika started cleaning up the patio for the dinner guests.

I even fully intended to walk out with my family when they took Kelty to my place to spend some family time, but then I saw Steve duck into the bathroom. I told Dad I had to check on something and would be right along, before I followed my friend into the men's room.

"Who, Mika? Well, yeah. She's my sister's best friend. They've been thick as thieves since elementary school. How do you think she ended up here?"

I walk in and lean against the counter. "What do you mean, ended up here?"

Steve wipes his hands and faces me full-on, crossing his

arms over his chest. "I recommended your cottage to her. Is there something I'm missing?"

He seems genuinely puzzled, but then so am I. "I don't know if you are, but I sure am."

"You're gonna have to give me more than that, buddy. I don't understand, I thought I was doing her and you both a favor by referring her. She needed a place to stay to catch her breath, I thought you'd be happy having a single tenant for the entire season, and now I hear she's even working for you —what's the problem?"

I rub my hands through my hair. Everything I learn about her just adds to my list of questions. "Nothing, it's just...a weird coincidence, that's all."

"What is?"

"When she ended up here, it was the third time we saw each other. I'm pretty sure she wasn't expecting me any more than I was expecting her."

"You already knew her?" His eyebrows shoot up.

"By seeing her. I bumped into her twice at Tufts Hospital."

"Ah, now that makes sense. Her son was at Tufts around the same time Kelty was there."

"I know. The first time I saw her was just after her boy died, in the hallway. She was a mess."

Steve grunts as his face turns hard. "That doesn't surprise me, that douchewipe of an ex of hers almost cost her the only positive she might be able to hold onto from Jamie's death. What an idiot."

His words tumble around in my brain, and suddenly a lot of pieces look like they might fit. "Positive?" I manage on a croak.

"Well, yeah. He'd been brain-dead for a week, the doctors already told her that time was running out because of cell degeneration."

"Running out on?" I ask, but I already know the answer. I know.

Steve suddenly drops his arms and leans forward, as I watch shocked realization wash over his features.

"No fucking way."

Mika

THE MOMENT I realized Steve wasn't here for me but for Jude, his college buddy, I knew I was living on borrowed time.

When I watch the two walk out of the men's room, I know it's too late.

Jude's head hangs low as he stalks straight out the front door without saying a word. Steve's gaze is focused on me and I feel a hot blush crawl up my neck.

"Sweetheart," is all he says and I shake my head.

"I can't now," I whisper, before he says anymore. "We have customers. I just can't."

"You know," Steve persists.

I put a pleading hand in the middle of his chest. "Please, Steve…not now."

He hesitates a moment before finally conceding with a nod. "All right, sweetheart, but I'm calling my sister."

"Steve…"

"No argument, Mika. I may have just lit a fuse, and you're gonna need her at your back when it blows up."

I don't get a chance to argue when a group of six walks in the door, and Steve slips out before I can stop him.

It takes everything out of me to smile and take orders, but apparently, I'm not doing such a great job hiding the turmoil inside, because when things slow down, Mandy pulls me aside.

"What's going on with you? You've been like a robot all night. Trouble in paradise?" she teases, wiggling her eyebrows, but instead of making me laugh, I feel the first tears spill over. "Oh shit," she mumbles. She rounds the bar, grabs me by the wrist, and starts pulling me down the hall. "Melissa! Take the bar for me. Emergency," she yells when we pass the kitchen. She drags me right into Jude's office, shutting the door behind us. "What on earth, Mika?"

It's like opening a can that's been shaken for a too long, there's just no way to stop the flow.

I barely notice Mandy shoving me down on a chair before disappearing out the door. A few moments she's back, dumping an industrial-sized roll of toilet paper on the floor in front of me.

"Typical fucking man, not having a single tissue anywhere," she grumbles, pushing a wad in my hand. "You're scaring me. Should I call Jude?"

"No! Please, I…I'll b-be fine."

We both know I'm lying, since my crying is turning hysterical.

"I'm getting you a stiff one."

"I d-don't d-drink," I stammer.

"You're fucking drinking tonight." She disappears again and I fight to get myself under control, only partially succeeding. "Here," she barks, shoving something so potent it stings my nose at me. "Don't think, just toss it back."

I do as she says, which triggers a coughing bout that works sobering. "Talk or I'm calling him," Mandy threatens when I take too long.

"I had a son," I start, and she immediately puts a hand on my arm.

"I know, Mika. I recognized your name before we even met. I'm so sorry you lost him."

"So you read about me?"

She doesn't look me in the eye. "I may have seen some stuff online, yeah."

I snort. "Bet it was enlightening," I can't help snap. Knee-jerk response.

"Actually one article was," she says in a serious voice. "It drew my attention because of the headline; "*Malice or Mercy*." It talked about your court case and quoted some examples of similar cases and their outcomes."

"Problem with every article out there, good or bad," I stop her, so tired of everything, "is that none of them includes all the information. This was about so much more than just my son's life. There wouldn't have been any urgency if that was the only consideration."

"I don't get it."

"Jamie was a good kid, a good friend to his buddies, a great son to me. He was generous to a T, and was quick to lend a helping hand. He would've wanted his death to mean something. I was determined to give him that, to give him a chance to live on. Time was running out and my ex didn't see things my way. My only option was to take him to court so I could let Jamie go, but save his organs."

"Oh Lord." Her hand presses against her chest. "Kelty."

"Yes. Kelty. I swear I had no idea," I hurry to add. "At least not until I recognized Jude walking up to the cottage. It's all such a mess." I grab another wad of paper from the roll and mop at my face. "It's been a series of coincidences I can't even begin to explain. The day Jamie died; I bumped into a stranger in the hallway who was unexpectedly kind to me. I saw him again at a fundraiser at the hospital in early May, when he talked about his daughter who had received a heart transplant. I recognized him and knew; I just knew his daughter had Jamie's heart. I ran out of there."

"Jesus." Mandy sniffles and rips off a length of toilet paper herself. "But wait. The first time you called about the cottage was the end of April. You said you were looking at a few other options."

"Yes, my best friend, Sam, gave me your number. Her brother is a Cape Cod real estate agent."

"Steve." She looks at me, her mouth hanging open. "Do you realize how fucked up this is?"

"Oh, yeah. I do. I swear, Mandy, I didn't plan this. I just got…swept up and then Jude kissed me."

"Jude? You haven't told him, have you?" I turn away when I see the accusation in her eyes.

Oh my God, what a mess. I can't help wonder why our paths seemed destined to cross at every turn, if it was going to end up like this anyway.

"I told him I was keeping something from him. I promised after Kelty's birthday I would tell him. He would've told me to leave, and I just wanted to be part of her birthday."

"Then Steve showed up," Mandy concludes correctly.

"And then Steve showed up," I agree.

"You have to talk to him."

I get up and start pacing the small office. "I don't know, Mandy."

"You owe him that."

Ouch.

She's right, though, he deserves to hear it from me, but not tonight.

"Tomorrow," I promise, but she seems less than

impressed. "Mandy, I'm raw, and I bet Jude is too. Tomorrow," I repeat firmly.

"Okay, but—"

The door opens and Melissa sticks her head inside. "Sorry to disturb but, Mika, your phone was behind the bar and has been ringing nonstop for the past five minutes." She holds out my phone and I take it from her.

Twelve missed calls from Sam's number in five minutes. That has to be a record.

"It's my friend, Sam," I begin to explain when the phone starts ringing again.

"Go," Mandy says, waving me out the door. "Go home. Get some rest, but tomorrow…" She wags an admonishing finger in my face.

"Tomorrow," I confirm. "I swear."

"Steve's an idiot."

It's the first thing out of Sam's mouth when I answer as I'm walking through the restaurant. I wave distractedly at Melissa and Penny on my way out the door.

"It's not his fault."

"He's my brother, of course it is."

"It's such a mess, Sam. I made such a mess of things." The tears that had mostly dried up start flowing again, as I walk up to the cottage and sit down on the top step. I glance over at the main house. It looks like his family is still there, judging from the extra cars remaining in the driveway.

"Say the word, babe," Sam says softly. "I can be out there in a couple of hours. Or you can come here if you feel up to driving."

"It's tempting," I sniffle. "But I've done enough running, Sam. This time I'm staying. It's the right thing to do, at least until I've talked to him."

"You like him."

"More than I should, given the circumstances," I admit, suddenly bone-weary and freezing cold. "I need to go inside, Sam. I'm exhausted."

"Okay. Call me anytime."

"I know. I don't know what I would've done without you. Love you bunches."

"You're a walking disaster, my friend, but I love you too."

I hang up, head inside, and in the dark almost trip over the four other frames I had mounted. I stumble straight to the small bathroom, flip on the lights, and strip down, not even bothering to pick up my clothes.

Letting the hot water pelt on my back, the cold that invaded my bones over the past hour slowly disappears. By the time I roll into bed, still wrapped in a towel, I can't even form a rational thought.

I'm emotionally drained.

Jude

I WATCH from the window as she comes walking out of the restaurant, her phone to her ear.

Steve's already gone. He popped by on his way out, but he picked up on my unwillingness to talk pretty quickly. He said his goodbyes and left.

My brother is gathering up his family right now, ready to head out. They're about half an hour north of Boston, so they won't be home before midnight as it is.

Kelty fell asleep on the couch next to her grampa, who's been nodding off as well. I'll get both of them to bed as soon as Ethan's gone.

"Sure you're okay, Jude?" he asks for the second time. I've done my best to put on a normal face, but he knows me well.

"Just some stuff I need to deal with tomorrow. I'll be fine."

"Okay. We're ready to get out of your hair. Was good seeing Kelty so much better, man. Happy she's doing so well."

I return his one-armed hug, kiss Libby, and share fist bumps with the boys before walking them out.

I'm still standing in my driveway when their taillights disappear. My gaze drifts to the cottage and I notice the bathroom light is the only one on. Is she still up?

It's probably a good thing I have to get my daughter to bed, or I might be tempted to go knock on her door. I'm still trying to rein in my emotions so it's probably best I don't.

Inside I say good night to Dad, get Kelty to bed, and after tidying up and turning off the lights, head upstairs myself.

Instead of turning on the lights in my bedroom, I walk straight over to the window and peek over at the cottage. It's completely dark. She must've gone to bed.

I strip, and slip between the covers, without bothering to brush or wash up.

Right now I'm beyond caring.

Chapter Twelve

Jude

IT'S amazing how quiet it can get here.

Before Kelty came to stay with me, I used to be up at the crack of dawn for my daily run. My hand inadvertently goes to my stomach, which I've noticed is getting soft. If I'm not careful, I'll end up with a gut like Dad, and more recently Ethan.

The gravel of the parking lot crunches under my shoes as I make my way to the cottage.

She's up. I saw the lights flick on inside a few minutes ago.

It's been a restless night, my brain unable to shut off long enough to reach a proper sleep, and I know today will be long. Longer still, if we don't clear the air.

I'm not looking forward to the conversation ahead. I don't expect it to be an easy one, but it's a necessary one. This whole situation has me freaked out. Conflicted. Suddenly unsure of the source for the feelings I started developing for her. Disturbed by the sequence of events that brought her here. Angry to be confronted with the reality of something I wasn't ready to deal with yet: Kelty's new heart once belonged to someone no longer here. And surprisingly enough, hurt at the possibility the connection I thought I felt with her might quite easily not have been real.

I tried to reason my way through this all night long, but there doesn't seem to be an easy way. So the hard way it is, with nerves raw and vulnerably exposed.

Maybe that's why I'm dragging my feet, taking my time making it to her steps. I've never been one who deals well with emotion, in particular my own. Yet I know talking with Mika will evoke many of them, for as many reasons.

This is one fucked-up situation, but it's not one I feel I can run from. Too much is at stake for too many people who mean a lot to me.

I take a seat on the top step and sip coffee from the travel mug I carried with me, waiting for her to come outside like she seems to do every morning.

"You're early," her soft voice sounds behind me, and I turn my head to see her standing over me, her hair a tangled mess, and her face still showing evidence of her own rough night.

In a silent invitation I scoot over, making room for her on the step, which she reads and accepts.

Despite the world of uncertainty hanging between us, I like the feel of her thigh brushing mine.

"Did you sleep?" I ask, my first words gravelly.

"Not much," she admits, taking a sip from the same cup I've seen her use before. "I knew this would be a hard conversation no matter what, but I want you to know I never meant for you to find out this way."

"I know."

"As much as I feel I had no control over what landed me in your life, that part I should've managed better, and I regret it deeply. I'm sorry, Jude. So very sorry."

I glance over and notice her fighting tears. Almost inadvertently, I reach out and tuck a strand of hair behind her ear. "I know," I repeat softly.

It's true, I know in my bones she didn't set out to hurt anyone. I believe we're both victims of some cruel cosmic joke we don't have the punch line to.

"It's funny," I admit. "I had so many questions, and for some reason, sitting here with you, I can't think of a single one to ask."

"Then let me talk. Let me tell you what I'd planned to tell you today anyway. If it brings up questions then ask, and I promise I'll answer. All of it."

I turn my head and catch her liquid blue eyes on me, swirling with emotions, open and unguarded. "Okay."

Listening to her talk about her son is difficult, as she rips that wound wide open so she can bleed—for me. The accident, taking a leave of absence to look after him, the growing tension between her and Jamie's father, and the last week of Jamie's life. I understand now why she fought to gain full control over her son. Why she didn't hesitate to 'pull the plug before the ink was dry' as my father put it. As a parent, I understand the need to give the inevitable death of your child value. Make it meaningful. Heck, Cassie and I had discussed some of these things ourselves during the months leading up to Kelty's heart transplant. Needing to find a purpose for the devastation of your loss.

It all makes sense.

"I didn't do well after Jamie died," she shares. "Emmett and his family were intent on vilifying me, I continued to be hounded by the press when I just wanted to be left alone. I'm not proud of sinking as low as I did—Jamie would've been so disappointed—but I got through somehow. Unfortunately, with the realization I had no clue what to do next, how to fill my life back up."

"Then you ended up here."

She smiles at my words, but her eyes never leave the water. "Yeah. The first time Kelty visited me I had no clue, but then you walked up. I'd heard you talk about your daughter at the fundraiser, and I just knew my son's heart was beating in your daughter's chest. I ran from the hospital as fast as I could, but when I saw you again, and realized Kelty was the daughter you'd spoken of, I felt like maybe I'd been given a gift."

"How is that?" My tone is sharp. Probably because I sense she's getting to the core of her motivations, and I'm afraid I might not like hearing them.

This time, it's her reaching for me. She slides her hand, palm up, under mine and curls her fingers to hold on. "In that moment, I thought as long as no one found out, there would be no harm done." A wave of anger has me pull at my hand, but she only grabs it tighter. "I was wrong, I didn't take into account the draw I had to you from the start. The feelings that would develop so quickly."

"In that you're not alone," I confess.

"I think I realize that. I want you to know, I'm so grateful having had this amazing opportunity to learn that when hope ends for one, life begins for another. To see for myself the good Jamie left behind in your daughter. To get to know both of you. I will never regret a moment of it. "

I pull my hand free and twist to face her. "That sounds like goodbye," I force myself to say.

"I think it's better for everyone if I leave."

I hate how reasonable she sounds, so I bark, "Why?"

"Because this kind of information is obviously hard to contain once out there. Because as long as my ex keeps talking to the press, sooner or later, they will find me here, and when they do they'll find Kelty as well. The only reason Emmett hasn't mentioned anything about Jamie's organs, having been donated, is because it doesn't suit his purpose to paint me as an evil mother and himself as a hapless victim. The reason I haven't brought it up to defend myself is because the media would have done their best to dig up the names of the organ recipients. The fallout wouldn't just be for Kelty, but for whomever has his kidneys, his liver, his corneas…the list goes on."

I pull myself up and run my hands through my hair as I walk down the steps. There I turn back to her. "Stay."

Her eyes brim with tears. "But the risk is—"

"Every day you get out of bed is a risk. You and I know better than most how true that is. Whether you're here, or somewhere else, won't make a difference once the truth is out there. If they dig they could still find us, and all those other families. Leaving won't serve any purpose." I've been pacing back and forth, but on my last words I stop and face her.

"I don't know what the smart thing is to do."

She wrings her hands in her lap and her teeth are biting her bottom lip so hard I'm afraid she'll break the skin.

I'll examine why it's so important to keep her here later, but for now I place my hands on the stair railing to brace myself, and lean forward, my nose almost touching hers.

"Stay."

Mika

. . .

"WHAT ABOUT THAT?"

I follow the direction Kelty is pointing. The remnants of a fishing net are tangled around a piece of driftwood where the last wave is just receding, leaving the sand even and smooth.

I didn't expect I'd still be here, but the force of Jude's determination I stay held a promise I wanted to grab onto. It helped that he reassured me, right before he left, we would talk through any issues that popped up, but there was no rush at this point.

Kelty surprised me just twenty minutes after her dad left, coming over to ask if I could help her with her camera. That led to her coming with me to the beach. As did her grandfather, who sat stoically beside me in the passenger seat, grumpy as ever. I don't know whose idea it was for him to come, but given the circumstances I wasn't about to complain. In any event, he's sitting on a bench at the edge of the parking lot, keeping an eye on his granddaughter roaming the beach below.

"That would make a great shot, but instead of aiming right at it and clicking, try to push the button just a little until you see that box appear in your viewfinder. The camera will automatically focus on anything that shows in the box and keep it like that as long as you don't move your finger. Then you carefully move the camera, just a little, so the wood isn't in the middle, but more on the side."

"Oops," she says when I hear the shutter click. "I pressed too hard."

I grin at her. "That's the beauty of digital pictures, it doesn't matter whether you try once or a hundred times, you can just keep trying until you get it right and delete the rest."

She tries again and this time she seems happy with the result when she checks her display. "Is this right?"

I take a peek. All that is visible is the perfectly smooth

sand with the driftwood coming in from the right side, making for a more interesting composition. "Right on the nose," I tell her, handing back the camera. "Want to try something cool?"

"Yeah."

"Remember I showed you that button where you can switch from close-ups all the way to landscapes, depending on what it is you aim the camera at? There's a setting on there with a little flower beside it."

"The one that says *micro*?"

"Exactly. Set it to micro and aim the camera at my hand." I hold my hand just a few inches from the lens. "You know what a microscope does, right?"

"It makes things look bigger," she confirms.

"Well, yes, but more importantly it make the tiniest things visible. Take a look in your viewfinder, what do you see?"

"Lines, and hair, little holes."

"And what do you see now?" I pull my hand from under the lens and hold it up to her when she lowers the camera. She pulls it closer to her face.

"I can see the lines, but barely."

"Exactly. Now let's have a close look at those rocks." I point at an outcropping that's hidden by the sea when the tide is high, covered in algae.

I'm not sure how much time has passed when I notice Kelty's yawn. I check my watch and see it's a lot later than I thought.

I wrap my arm around her shoulder and lead her back to where Jim has dozed off, his head tilted back, on the bench.

"Grampa, have a look."

She giggles when he snorts awake, but he patiently sits through the thirty or so pictures Kelty took. "You did good, Peanut," he says, kissing the top of her head.

Just like that, I feel any negative emotions I have toward the man slip quietly into the background. It's obvious he dotes on his granddaughter.

The drive home is quiet without Kelty's enthusiasm filling the air. I check the mirror to find her slumped in the back seat, her eyes drifting shut. When I pull into the parking lot, and turn the engine off, I'm surprised to find Jim facing me.

"Going out again tomorrow?" he asks, almost flooring me.

"If the weather is good."

"What time?"

"Probably around nine," I answer, not sure what to make of this.

"If the sun is out, we'll be ready."

Without another word he gets out, helps Kelty out of the back seat, and walks her to the main house, while I'm still behind the wheel, figuring out what to make of him.

Apparently my solo trips to the beach have become a group affair.

Chapter Thirteen

Jude

I'M STANDING by my office window when I see Mika's car return, and like almost every day this past week, my dad lifts himself out of the passenger seat and opens the back door for Kelty.

This has become their daily routine; one my father seems to have settled into as easily as Kelty has. To say it surprised me would be an understatement, as far as Dad's concerned. It's not like he was a fan of Mika, but it almost seems like he's warming up to her. Ever since Kelty's birthday.

I've been keeping my distance since my early morning heart-to-heart with Mika. Not because I'm still upset, but because now that I know where we both stand, I'm not sure how to move forward.

Cassie is the first person I've thought about telling. She deserves to know what's going on as much as I do. What's holding me back is the concern that Cassie may have her own ideas about having Mika connecting with our daughter.

I'm being a coward, hanging onto this status quo, and I know it. I've seen Mika's questioning glances in my direction, and I know she's waiting for my lead. My problem is any move I make, anything I do, might have consequences I can't foresee, prevent, or control.

On top of that, it looks like Kelty is pretty worn out again, something that has me a little concerned. I've got to make sure to mention it to the cardiologist at her six-month checkup in a few days.

"Did you call the supplier yet?" Mandy asks, when I walk through the restaurant on my way to check on my daughter.

"What?"

"You were supposed to call in that liquor order, or we won't get it in time for the weekend."

Shit. I totally forgot. "I'll do it now."

"No, I'll do it," Mandy snaps. "At least that way I know it'll get done."

"Fuck. I'm sorry, I haven't had my head in the game."

"No, you haven't," she confirms, never one to mince words. "It's been up your ass."

"Now hold on a minute…"

"You know I'm right, Boss." She steps in my space and lowers her voice. "I don't wish what you have on your plate on anyone, but for God's sake, step away and take some time to sort it. You're not helping anyone if you're here, but you aren't really. And it's contagious, because Mika can't focus when you're around either."

"It's not that easy…" I let my voice trail off, because whatever I would've spouted after is just an excuse.

"I get that. I *get* it. I'm probably the only one who does. Who do you think dealt with Mika after you stormed out of here on your daughter's birthday? I *know*, and I'm telling you as a friend, get this sorted.

Right now you're just holing up in your office, waiting for the other shoe to drop. Get ahead of the game, Jude."

It's rare that Mandy calls me by my name, so I know she's dead serious. She's right too.

Instead of getting pissed, I hook her around the neck, pull her into a hug, and kiss the top of her head. "You're a good friend."

She immediately wrestles from my hold and fake shivers as she addresses the ceiling, "Jesus, now he's going soft on me. Get outta here."

The house is quiet when I walk in, and I wonder if Dad went to lie down too. Kicking off my shoes, I make my way upstairs to Kelty's room to find my father sitting on the edge of her bed, watching her.

"She okay?" I look down on my daughter, who looks like she's already fast asleep.

"Yeah," he says a little hesitantly before getting to his feet. "Let's let huh sleep."

I follow Dad downstairs and into the kitchen. "Did she have lunch?"

"No, she was asleep on huh feet when we got back. I'll make something when she wakes up." He pulls the makings for a sandwich from the fridge and sets it on the counter. "You gonna eat, or aw ya headin' back?"

"Mandy kicked me out."

His eyes lock on mine. "She sick of ya mopey ass too?"

Guess I've been more obvious than I thought I was. "Something like that," I mumble.

"Mmmm." I watch silently as he slaps together a couple of sandwiches and shoves one my way. "She's not that bad," he says, his mouth full.

"Who? Mika?" I guess.

"Mmmm. Treats my granddaughtah like gold," he says, taking another bite.

I set my sandwich down and take a deep breath. It's the perfect opening. "Mika cares about her. A lot. She has reason to."

His looks up at me. "That so?"

"Yeah. Those stories you heard—the ones going around about her—they don't tell the whole story. Mika fought for her son to be taken off life support so his organs wouldn't deteriorate before they could be harvested." I see awareness come into his expression. "His outcome was inevitable, but she wanted to give his death meaning."

"Kelty?" he whispers, putting his own sandwich down on the plate before pulling over a stool and sinking down.

I simply nod, giving him a moment to absorb that before I start at the beginning. Lunch sits untouched, all but forgotten by the time I finish.

"You like huh."

"It's complicated, Dad."

"Bullcrap. Nothin' in life worth anything is easy. Ya problem's always been wantin' to know the next step, instead of trustin' ya feet will land eventually. If this past yeah should've taught you anything, it's that sometimes you gotta just grab on and have a little faith."

"I thought you didn't like her?"

He shrugs, picking up his sandwich and taking a bite before he responds with his mouth full. "Now ah do."

"That simple?" I question him but he just shrugs.

"She's the reason ah still have my peanut? Then hell yeah, that simple."

Mika

AFTER CLEARING AWAY the remnants of lunch, I'm just sitting down to upload this morning's pictures when my phone rings.

"Bryan, I hope you have good news?"

I smile at my realtor's responding deep chuckle.

"I might," he teases. "That is, if you consider a bidding war good news."

"What?"

"Did an open house last weekend, like I told you, and had a great turnout. So good, I had two couples setting up a subsequent walk-through, one after the other, and both their agents contacted me with numbers."

"Good numbers?" I ask hopefully.

"At this point, between the two bidders, we're sitting fifteen grand over asking."

"You're kidding!" I grin wide. I'd been prepared to settle for that amount less than the listing price, so this is an unexpected potential boost of thirty thousand dollars.

"Not even a little. The only difference between the two offers is that one is looking for a closing September first, and the other couple is currently renting so they'd like a closing of mid-July, so they can be moved in before their lease expires the end of that month."

"The sooner the better," I quickly answer, barely able to contain my excitement.

Working at the Cooker helps, as do the free meals, but the sale of my house will set me up for whatever I end up wanting to do, without worrying about my basic needs. I have some ideas, especially after stopping by The Cape PhotoArt & Framing. The guy running that place was very helpful, and he did a great job on my prints. With the money from the house I'll be able to move from toying with ideas to seriously exploring my options.

"When can you come into town?"

"Whenever, I may need to shuffle a few things here, but I'm sure I can make it happen. Mornings are better."

"How are you enjoying the Cape, by the way?"

"I love it here. A completely different pace than Boston. I used to love the hustle and bustle of the city, but I have to say, at this age, I'm enjoying this more laid-back vibe."

"So can I take that to mean we won't see you back on the tube?"

"I haven't quite figured out what it is I'll be doing, but I can assure you it will not be in front of a camera." I realize as I'm saying this how true it is. I don't really care if it's waiting tables the rest of my life, or something else, but I'll never rejoin a profession that can turn on you as quickly as it did on me.

"I hear you on that," Bryan rumbles with understanding, and I'm warmed to realize I still have some friends left in this world. "So I'll set something up and text you with a time. Sound good?"

"Perfect."

The moment I hang up my smile slides from my face.

I sold my house. The place where I was happy in a previous life, but the memories are painful now. The walls that still echo the disgruntled cries of a newborn baby boy in such a hurry to make an appearance, we never quite made it to the hospital. The kitchen counter, where he'd sit in his high chair, feeding me half his Cheerios with his wide tooth-less smile. The stairs he fell down, crying uncontrollably until I kissed the bump on his head better. The twelve marks on the kitchen wall, recording how much he'd grown up with every passing birthday. And even the split doorframe, the result of a slammed door during his first adolescent tantrum.

All of those things had become like sandpaper to my emotions, keeping me raw and mourning. It's also the place where Sam found me, one morning earlier this year, almost lost to the shadows surrounding me. That wasn't a testament to Jamie; it was an insult. The once happy house had turned into a trap I couldn't get out of. Until I did.

Things, places, and even people aren't memories—feelings are.

I don't realize I'm crying until a knock sounds at my door and I open it to find Jude on my step.

"*Fuck*. What happened?"

He rushes me inside, closes the door, and pulls me close, pressing my face in his neck.

"I sold my house," I mumble against his skin, and he immediately loosens his hold. I tilt my head back and look in his confused face.

"And here I was, thinking that would be good news," he quips with an eyebrow raised, but concern in his eyes.

"It is," I confirm, turning out of his arms and waving in the direction of the Keurig as I head toward the bathroom. "Make yourself a coffee, I'm just going to clean up."

By the time I've splashed some water on my face and walk out, he's sipping fresh brew while leaning against the counter. Immediately he sets his cup down and meets me halfway, slipping his arms around my waist. I brace my hands against his chest.

"Wanna tell me what that was about?"

"Letting go."

He scans my face with his eyes. "Jamie," he finally says, with a depth of understanding only a parent having gone through his own version of hell could feel.

"Yeah," I confirm. "I had to let it go to move forward, let his memory free instead of leaving it locked in brick and mortar."

"You won't forget," he promises, lifting a hand to stroke my hair, "You'll keep him here…" before moving his palm to press between my breasts, "…and here."

The feel of his large hand on my chest has a flush rise to my cheeks, and my heart beats a staccato against his palm.

"What brings you here?" I ask, the sound almost breathless around the lump in my throat.

"You. I want you." He doesn't bother hiding the hunger in his eyes, which is both exhilarating and more than a little frightening. "All I've been doing is thinking. Fuck, I've been thinking so hard my head hurts. I've always been one to trust in facts and figures. To process information until I could line it all up in my head. But I'll be damned if I can make sense of this with any logic or formula or even rationale. There is none, I've tried. What's left are feelings, and as my dad reminded me just now, sometimes you just have to grab on and have faith."

Lord, this man is lethal, not only with his lips and hands, but his words too.

"Your dad?" I clue in on what he just said.

"Mmmm. Got a stern talking to when I shared with him how much exactly we owe you—owe Jamie," he quickly amends.

"You don't owe anything," I remind him softly, but he shakes his head.

"You're wrong," he says firmly, his head lowering so his lips brush mine softly. "We owe you and your son our world."

Chapter Fourteen

Jude

THE KISS STARTS SOFT, tentative.

I still have a hand on her lower back and the other between the soft swells of her breasts. It wasn't meant to be a sexual touch, but with the hitch of her breath at the slightest brush of my lips, and her rapid heartbeat under my hand, it's where this moment is taking us.

I angle my head slightly and lick along the seam of her mouth. Immediately she opens to let me in, as her hands slide from my chest up and around my neck, the subtle shift inviting me to stroke my palm over her breast. She groans in response and hardens underneath my thumb when I lightly brush her nipple.

She smells like the beach, and it's easy to get lost in the feel of her body, the taste of her mouth. Almost instinctively, my already rock-hard shaft pushes against her gently rounded belly.

Hungry to feel the silk of her skin, I slip my hand from her lower back down the waistband of her shorts to cover one smooth, pliable asscheek. My turn to groan as her tongue tangles with mine.

I start walking her back toward the couch, but before we get there her nails dig into my neck, and she rips her mouth from mine.

"What are we doing?"

"Making out." My mouth immediately aims to recapture hers but she turns her head away. I note her hands are still hanging onto me.

"I start at four."

"Two hours is enough for starters," I counter, guessing at the time.

"Jude…" she moans when I squeeze the globe of her lush behind. "I need to shower and change."

"I can work with an hour and a half."

With her head still turned, I have no choice but to drag my lips from her cheek to her strong jawline. She lifts her chin, inviting me to slide my mouth down the slim column of her neck. I latch onto the soft skin where it meets her shoulder and start moving her backward again.

When we reach the couch, I set both my hands on her hips, twist us around, and land on my back, Mika draped on top of me.

"What are we doing here?" she asks again, her chin propped up on her folded hands on my chest and her eyes inquisitive.

I slide my hands under her shirt, finding the soft skin of her back. "Exploring." It's the only way I know how to answer her.

"Me or us?"

I grin at her. "Both, since one leads to the other. Although

I already can pretty much guarantee we're about as compatible as you can get. Fuck, Mika, just about everything about you turns me on. There's no denying this chemistry, so don't even try."

A little self-satisfied smile tilts the corners of her mouth up as she lowers her eyes. "Sure of yourself."

I pull a hand from her shirt and bring it up to cup her face, my thumb under her chin to lift it. "When it comes to this I am. I may not understand why, but this thing between you and me has been leading to this point from the start."

"Yeah," she agrees mumbling, as she presses her face to the hollow of my neck.

My hand tangles in her hair and I let myself enjoy the weight of her on top of me. I'd love nothing more than to strip her naked, and bury myself so deep I can't tell where I end and she begins, yet somehow lying with her like this— our clothes on but emotionally exposed—feels much more intimate.

My fingers draw mindless circles on her scalp, and every now and then she almost purrs like a kitten. Sounds that make it hard to ignore my body's response to her.

"Don't stop," she says, when I pull my hand from her hair.

"Self-preservation, baby. Much more of those little mewls of yours, and I'm afraid I'll be fucking you on this couch, and I won't care anyone can see in the window."

She chuckles softly before lifting her face just inches from mine. "There's always the bedroom." This time it's me making the pathetic little sounds as she tortures me with the heat her eyes. "I left the blinds closed this morning."

A man can only take so much before he acts.

She giggles when I roll us off the couch and onto our feet, and carry-walk her into the open door of her bedroom and straight to her bed. I let go only to rip my shirt over my head and undo the button on my jeans. Without hesitation, Mika does the same, revealing a simple white bra cupping her breasts and I instinctively reach out, lift them, and bury my face in the resulting cleavage. Not ample, but more than enough to fill my hands and senses.

"You're beautiful," I mumble against her skin and I can feel her laugh.

"How can you tell, you haven't even seen me yet," she teases.

This is a new experience for me, this playfulness in the bedroom. A light atmosphere in which insecurities that come with getting naked with someone for the first time have no place.

"I'm going to rectify that now," I warn her, lifting my face and slipping my hands around her back to undo the clasp on her bra.

Her eyes are a mesmerizing combination of humor and heat, and I can't break away from them, even as I slowly expose those glorious breasts. Our eyes stay locked, while our hands bump, suddenly in a hurry to divest ourselves of the remainder of our clothes.

It's not until she sits down on the edge of the bed and scoots back onto the mattress that I break the hold of her gaze to take in the rest of her body. All creamy skin and lush curves. Her breasts full with deep pink aureoles pinched tight into firm peaks. A hit of ribs leading down to a softly rounded belly, criss-crossed with thin white lines in memory of the child she carried there. Wide, sturdy hips framing a darker blonde thatch of hair before stretching into a pair of solid but shapely legs.

"You're beautiful," I repeat my earlier words. This time

she doesn't laugh, but her smile is lazy and warm as she lets her own eyes take me in.

Taking my engorged cock in hand, I squeeze lightly just under the crown in an effort to slow myself down before putting a knee in the bed. She lets her legs drop open, making room for me there and revealing her slick, deep rose pussy. My nostrils flare, taking in the warm scent of her arousal. The urge to slide myself inside that heat almost overwhelming.

"Fuck," I grind out between clenched teeth with the sudden realization I came unprepared.

Mika

MY GOD HE'S GORGEOUS.

Real.

Wide shoulders, salt-and-pepper hair lightly covering a well-shaped chest, and narrowing into a straight line down his stomach to the thick, almost purple, shaft jutting from the dark nest of curls between two solid, strong thighs. No countable abs, no bulging muscles, but with a body as real as my own—except all man.

"Come here," I whisper when he curses softly, eager to get my hands on him.

He lifts his eyes and I see the regret. "I don't have anything. No condom."

I let my hand slide down my stomach and run my finger along the thin line bisecting me hip to hip. His eyes follow hungrily.

"Hysterectomy." His gaze flies up to mine, and I swear I

see a hint of pain there before heat takes over. "And I'm clean. It's...it's been a while," I confess.

"Same," he rumbles. "But are you sure?"

"Come here."

His eyes flutter closed as he takes in a deep breath, before climbing over me and slowly lowering his hips between my legs.

"I'm going to need hours to explore every inch of you."

"Next time," I assure him, tilting my hips.

"Promise?" The sudden insecurity in his voice tears at me, and I lift my hand to his jaw.

"Cross my heart," I whisper, my lips a breath away from his.

As he takes my mouth in a bruising kiss, I feel the broad crown of his cock probing at my entrance, and I pull my legs up higher. The stretch feels decadent, and almost too much, as he slides himself inside until there's no air left between his skin and mine.

The connection much deeper than just our bodies.

I explore his shoulders, back, and down to his ass, flexing under my hands with every surge of his hips. His head lifts and those brown eyes, dark with emotion, burn into mine, holding them even as his breath becomes ragged and his movements almost erratic. My fingers dig in and I buck up under him...reaching for my release.

Then I'm falling, my mouth wide, eyes closing, at the involuntary contractions of my body. I'm barely cognizant of the words tumbling from Jude's lips as he plants himself deep, jerking with his own release.

His face buried in my neck, I wrap myself around him, waiting for our breathing to slow down. I wish I could make time stop, and stay in this moment indefinitely. I whimper when I feel him slide softly from my body and his head lifts from my neck.

"It's gonna get messy," he warns, humor in his eyes.

For a minute I'm confused, until I feel his cum slipping out of me. "I need a shower."

Then he rolls off me, chuckling softly as I scoot out of bed and into the bathroom. I've barely hopped under the steady stream of water when the door opens, and I see his shape through the frosted shower door. Without inhibition, he relieves himself before sliding open the door and stepping in.

"Preserving water," he says by way of explanation, pressing a quick kiss on my lips before sudsing himself thoroughly with my light-scented buttermilk soap. "Gonna be hard all day long with your scent on me," he grumbles, making me smile.

For all the obvious complications that surround us, being with Jude is comfortable, effortless, and as natural as if we've been together forever.

Aside from sharing longing, appreciative glances, we manage to dry off and get dressed quickly.

"I should go," I remind him, stepping out on the porch, Jude following behind me and closing my door.

"Yeah. I should probably check in to see if Kelty's up yet."

His arm snakes around my middle and he tugs me close, ignoring the fact we're in full view not only of the restaurant, but the main house as well.

"They can see us," I caution him, but he only pulls me closer.

"I don't care," he mumbles right before his mouth closes over mine.

My hands come up and curl around his neck, amazed how

the mere touch of his tongue to mine can have the heat pooling in my lower belly, when I hear a voice calling.

"Jude! It's Kelty!"

One moment I'm melting in his arms, the next I have goosebumps rising all over my body as I watch Jude jump down the steps and sprint in the direction of his house, where his father is hanging over the railing.

No.

Chapter Fifteen

Jude

"WHERE IS SHE?"

I sound breathless, mostly because of the panicked pounding of my heart in my chest.

"Couch," Dad says, stepping aside to let me through. "She doesn't look right and feels hot to the touch, Son."

I lean over the couch to find my daughter with her eyes closed. Her face is white, droplets of perspiration on her forehead and upper lip, which is a worrisome purplish hue. Her breathing sounds labored.

"Dad, get a blanket and get in the back seat of my truck. We're driving her to Tufts."

"*Stop.*"

My head swings around at the sound of Mika's voice. I hadn't noticed her following me.

"We've gotta go."

"Stop and think, please. Calling an ambulance gets medical help here faster," she urges, taking a step closer.

"You're in no condition to drive and neither is your father. Please, think for a minute."

"I can't just wait around," I snap at her, scared out of my brain, but then she steps right up to me and puts a hand on my cheek. "Besides, the ambulance will take her to Hyannis or Falmouth, when she should be at Tufts."

"Call her cardiologist, he can advise over the phone, arrange for MedFlight to pick her up if necessary, but she needs medical attention *now*."

The next fifteen minutes are an anxious blur as we wait for the ambulance Mika called. I managed to get hold of Kelty's cardiologist, who immediately put me on hold to make arrangements for MedFlight to pick her up from a predetermined landing spot along Highway 6, where the ambulance will take her.

The ambulance crew's assurances, they've been in contact with her cardiologist, make it easier to get out of their way so they can get to my daughter, but I still stand frozen when they start wheeling her out of the house.

"Go. You may not be able to get on the flight, but you can stay with her in the ambulance," Mika says, squeezing my arm.

"I'll follow ya, Son," Dad adds, grabbing my car keys from the hook by the door, as he too urges me to follow the stretcher.

I vaguely register Mandy come running from the restaurant, but Mika intercepts her, and I climb into the back of the ambulance and sit down where the paramedic directs me.

"I need room to move around your daughter, so please stay in your seat."

I nod numbly and sit helplessly, my useless hands clutched in my lap.

"Jude?" I look at the open door to find Mika sticking her head in. "You need to call her mother. Call Cassie."

Then the door is slammed shut and moments later the ambulance takes off, sirens blaring. The full gravity of the situation threatens to crush me, when I remember Mika's instructions and pull my phone from my pocket.

I'm about to call Cassie's home number when a stray lucid thought has me call Mark's cell instead.

In as few words as possible, I explain what's happening in logistical terms, even though I have no idea myself what is going on with my daughter. Mark, as he's often been before, is calm and methodical, much like Mika was earlier, and promises me he'll find a way to get Cassie to Boston.

I lean my head back against the side of the ambulance, my fingers pressing into my eyes as I fight to keep control of my emotions.

"Daddy?"

My eyes shoot open at the sound of Kelty's voice. "Right here, Princess."

"I'm sorry," she says in a croaky voice as a tear rolls down her cheek. "I hoped it would go away."

All I can do is reach over and grab her little foot, while I press my lips together and try to smile at her blurring face.

———

"I'LL SEE YOU SOON, Princess. They'll take good care of you."

I give my daughter a quick kiss and have to stand by and watch as they slide her into the waiting helicopter.

Fear has a sharp, bitter taste, and it burns like acid in your veins.

Fear is also irrational, which is why—when I see Mika

behind the wheel of my approaching vehicle with Dad in the passenger seat beside her—I let loose.

"What the hell are you doing here?" I snap at her through clenched teeth.

Registering the shocked jerk of her body, I feel instant regret, but it's too late to call back my words. I'm not even sure why I'm lashing out at her.

To my surprise Dad steps between us, putting a restraining hand in my chest. "Easy, Son. Mandy told huh to drive. I was shakin' too bad." Shame joins fear. Suddenly dizzy, I lean forward into my father's chest, and his arms immediately wrap around me, holding me upright. "Best we get going. You good to drive, gal?"

"I'm good."

Fuck. Her voice is shaky, but I can hear determination, and it occurs to me she must be scared too.

I let my father lead me to the passenger side and climb in, remembering to buckle up. Dad climbs in the back and Mika fits herself behind the wheel. She looks too small for this truck as she fastens her seat belt as well, squares her shoulders, and starts the engine.

"Were you able to get hold of Cassie?" she asks softly, as she pulls onto the highway.

"Mark, her husband. He's been a rock this past year." My voice sounds empty, even to my own ears.

She reaches for my hand and slips her fingers between mine, holding on tight. "That's good, that you both had him."

I turn to her at the wistful tone in her voice, and realize she didn't have that. She had an ex-husband, who fought her and vilified her before, during, and after her son's death. She never had the kind of support Cassie and I have been blessed with, and yet here she is offering it to me.

I squeeze her hand and she glances my way.

"I'm sorry."

"I know," is her simple reply.

But it's not that simple, and I know it.

Mika

MOST OF THE ride into Boston is quiet.

I end up dropping Jude and his father off on Washington, right in front of the entrance, before I go hunting for a parking spot. When I find one, I slip the Traverse into the space and turn off the engine. Then I drop my forehead to the steering wheel and break down.

Deep, heaving, painful sobs tear from my chest and I don't even try holding back. I've been so focused on keeping my head for Jude, I haven't given myself the chance to be scared, and I'm terrified.

I don't know how long I sit like that when my cell buzzes in my purse. I wipe my face with my sleeve, pull it out and see Cooker on the screen.

"You were gonna call," Mandy says without hello.

"I will. I haven't even made it inside yet. I'm just parking the car."

"Are you crying?"

"I'm done," I tell her, sniffing loudly before I change the subject. "Were you able to get someone in?"

"We've got it covered here. Get your ass inside and get me an update."

"I will."

I twist the rearview mirror to check my face; glad I took the time to grab my purse, because my face is a mess. I pull a wet wipe from the travel-sized envelope and clean up as best I can. I'm still pretty blotchy when I get out of Jude's truck.

I click it shut, make note of the parking spot, and suddenly realize I'm kind of stuck as long as Jude is here. I'm not even sure how I will hold up inside the hospital, the fundraiser was in the lobby, and already I found it nearly unbearable.

After receiving a few odd looks, I unclip my hair to hide my face.

It takes me twenty minutes of wandering around before I find them in a waiting room near the pediatric ICU.

"I was about to come lookin' faw ya," Jim says when he spots me.

Jude jumps up and stalks over, pulling me roughly into his arms. "Worried maybe I chased you off."

I grab on his shirt in the small of his back and hold on.

"Any word?" I ask, lifting my head from his chest to look up in his face.

"Only that her cardiologist is with her now," he says, sounding drained. "They moved her straight to the ICU apparently, and are running tests to find out what's wrong. I'm hoping we'll be able to see her soon."

Behind me the door opens, hitting me in the back. I step out of the way and out of Jude's arms as his brother walks in.

"Sorry, Mika," he mumbles before taking a few steps toward his brother, giving him a quick hug. "Libby stayed with the boys for now. Any word?"

I go sit down beside Jim, while Jude repeats what he just told me, and am surprised when the older man pats my knee before he stands up to greet Ethan.

Waiting rooms are always awkward, and even though it's only us so far, it's no less strained now.

"Did you talk to Cassie?" Ethan asks, when Jude sits close on the other side of me.

"Mark. I talked to him, he says they're coming."

"I thought she was on forced bed rest?"

Jude snorts. "There's nothing that would keep her from her daughter."

"Guess not," his brother concedes before turning to me. "And you, Mika, how did you get here?"

"She drove us," Jim says for me, and I throw him a grateful smile.

"And she's with me," Jude says, grabbing my hand in between his.

Ethan looks down at our hands, then at each of us, but just as he opens his mouth to say something the door opens again.

A tall handsome man, with brown hair, I recognize from his publicity picture on the back of his books, wheels in a pretty blonde woman in a wheelchair. This has to be Cassie; her daughter is her spitting image. The moment she claps her eyes on Jude she bursts out crying. He's immediately up and out of his seat, dropping to his knees beside the chair and wraps her in his arms.

Her husband shoots me an apologetic smile over their heads before he bends down to them. "We're blocking the door, guys."

I grow increasingly uneasy, feeling out of place as the family exchanges hugs and greetings.

"Aren't you supposed to be in bed?" Ethan questions Cassie when he leans down to kiss her cheek. Her lips form a tight line as she glares at her husband.

"She should be," Mark says, ignoring his wife's angry look. "Which is why we'll be heading straight for maternity the moment after she's had a chance to see her daughter."

"You're a tyrant," she snaps, but he just grins and bends down, kissing the top of her head.

"I don't think we've met." Mark turns to me and holds out his hand. I take it, getting to my feet. "Mark Sommer," he introduces himself.

"I know," I say stupidly and immediately follow it up with, "I've read your books. Mika Spencer. I work for—"

"I know who you are too," he says with a smile. "I'm a bit of a sports fan, but even if I wasn't, Kelty's been talking you up."

At the mention of her name, I feel tears welling up. This isn't about Jamie's heart anymore; it's Kelty's heart now. That little girl has become very important to me in a short time, but it feels wrong to invade her family's privacy.

I should go; I don't belong here.

"Cassie," I hear Mark say, stepping aside for his wife. "This is Mika."

The smile she sends me is warm. "So you're the famous Mika. My daughter has a bit of a crush on you," she tells me.

"And she's not the only one," Jude announces, tucking his arm around my shoulders.

"Glad to meet you." I feel like such a fraud as I offer my hand. "Of course I wish it was anywhere but here."

"My daughter is strong, she'll be okay." Cassie pats my hand in hers when she notices the tears I'm willing back.

"Excuse me," I mumble, pulling my hand back and stepping out of Jude's hold. "I need to find a restroom."

With my eyes focused on my feet, I aim for the door, pull it open, bumping into solid barrel chest. Two firm hands grab my shoulders to keep me steady.

"I'm sorry, I wasn't...Ms. Spencer?"

I look up sharply at the familiar voice. "Dr. Cosgrove, I'm sorry, I wasn't looking."

"You know Kelty's cardiologist?" I hear Cassie saying behind me, and I know the ceiling is about to come down on me.

"I'm sorry," I mutter again as I squeeze by the doctor and rush down the hall, locking myself in the first bathroom I see.

Chapter Sixteen

Jude

SHIT.

I resist the urge to run after Mika as the door slowly closes on her retreating form.

Dr. Cosgrove looks confused from Cassie to me and back.

"I wasn't aware you knew—" he starts before I quickly cut him off.

"What's wrong with our daughter?"

He blinks a few times before collecting himself. "Right. It's not rejection. X-rays came back showing fluid in both her lungs. It looks like Kelty has contracted pneumonia. The lab is running cultures to see if it's viral or bacterial, but in the meantime, we have her on intravenous antibiotics. This is one of the risks we spoke about that are a side effect of the immunosuppressants, but we have to get this under control. So far her heart looks good, but we need to keep it that way."

"I don't understand, we've been so careful. She never showed any symptoms, other than getting tired a lot."

The cardiologist nods sympathetically. "She didn't voice any complaints, am I right?"

"Not to me," I confirm before turning to Mark and Cassie. "You?"

"Of course not," Cassie snaps, irritated.

"Doesn't surprise me," he says. "You'd be surprised how many seriously ill children try to be tough and downplay their symptoms for the sake of their parents. She knows how scared you were, how concerned you still are, and she doesn't want to be responsible for adding to it."

"*Jesus*," I hear Ethan hiss behind me.

I clearly remember Kelty's apology in the ambulance. It makes a lot more sense now.

"Can we see her?" Cassie asks.

"Give the nurses twenty minutes. Someone will come get you, but they're in the middle of a shift change. No more than two at a time in the ICU," he reminds us. "And not for long, she needs rest. I'll be in tomorrow morning to see if she's responding to the antibiotics, and we'll take it from there."

A chorus of thank-yous goes up when he leaves the room.

"Am I crazy to be relieved her body's not rejecting the heart?" Cassie asks.

"It was my biggest fear too, so no, not crazy," I assure her.

"Let's not crack open the champagne just yet," Mark, the voice of reason, contributes. "She has a weakened immune system and is battling double pneumonia. If it's viral, there's nothing antibiotics will do and her body will have to work to battle the infection by itself."

"Be right back," Dad says, slipping out of the room.

Shit, that's right, Mika.

"Did you bring that woman to Kelty's appointment?"

Clearly Cassie hasn't forgotten either, but leaps to the wrong conclusion.

"No," I tell her truthfully.

"That's some coincidence then." Her tone makes it clear she doesn't buy it. Ironically, it is exactly that. I have to squash the urge to go find Mika, and instead take in a deep breath. It's time for full disclosure.

"It is, actually. A crazy coincidence."

That's when I start telling her about the woman I saw crying in the hallway last December, and five minutes later I leave her a sobbing mess in Mark's arms when I head down the hallway to look for Mika.

I find her in the cafeteria, having a coffee with Dad at one of the small tables. Her eyes are worried when she spots me coming toward them.

Leaning down I kiss her forehead and pull up a chair from a neighboring table.

"Coffee, Son? Maybe you can talk huh into eating somethin'."

"Get a tray of coffees and some muffins or something, yeah, Dad? I'm sure the others can use some too, and we should get back to them."

I immediately feel tension coming off her.

"I didn't know—"

"I know you didn't," I tell her, taking her hand between mine. "It's fine." She doesn't look like she quite believes me but she'll find out soon enough.

"Your father tells me it's pneumonia?"

"Yeah. The heart's holding strong, though."

She drops her head to our clasped hands on the table, and I bend forward to shield her a little from the public eye while she quietly cries.

"We should head back," I nudge her gently, when I see

144

Dad trying to balance two trays of coffee and a large brown bag. "Before my dad spills a gallon of coffee on innocent bystanders," I add, and Mika's head shoots up. I nod in his direction and she follows my gaze.

We quickly go divest my father of the bulk of his load and make our way back to the PICU.

"Give me one second," Mika stops outside the ladies' room and hands me her tray before darting inside.

"Caught huh in the lobby. She was makin' faw the doaw."

"It's been an intense day. Plus, I imagine the hospital doesn't hold good memories for her. I'm only now starting to realize how traumatic this must be for her, Dad. If anything happened it would be like losing a child all over again. I don't know anyone who'd be strong enough to stay standing."

"Everything a'ight in theah?" He tips his head to the waiting room.

"Yeah, although it'd be a miracle if that baby doesn't decide to come early. I'm not taking any bets on Cassie's blood pressure."

Mika's strung tight as a bow when I push the waiting room door open, but the only one inside is Ethan.

"They're in with Kelty," Ethan clarifies, but his gaze is fixed on Mika. "A nurse just came to get them."

"Good." I point at one of the trays we set down on the table. "Grab a coffee."

"In a minute."

Before I realize what's happening, he has Mika wrapped in a bear hug, her feet dangling off the floor.

"Set her down, idiot," I snap when I see a flash of panic on her face. "You're gonna break her ribs."

Mika looks a little dazed when he sets her back on her feet, and Dad grabs for her arm when she teeters on her feet.

"I…I should call Mandy," she stammers, walking on wobbly legs to the purse she left on a chair earlier.

Ethan gives my shoulder a shove and we both reach for a coffee and sit down, Mika's soft voice as she gives Mandy an update the only sound in the room.

A little bit later, after I finally convinced her to eat one of the muffins Dad picked up, Mark pushes the wheelchair through the door. The instant Cassie's eyes lock on Mika, she bursts out crying again.

"I'm sorry, it's hormones," she explains, grabbing the wad of tissues Mark hands her before he walks over to Mika, bends down, and kisses her cheek.

"Thank you," I hear him say softly before he straightens and turns to me. "She's waiting for you."

I get to my feet and realize I'm faced with a dilemma when I meet Mika's eyes, but she almost imperceptibly shakes her head. I slide my fingers along her jaw, and lace them in her hair, tugging lightly to tilt her head back, before I plant a kiss on her mouth I hope conveys all I'd say if we were alone.

"Dad?" is all I need to say as I move to the door.

Right before it closes behind me, I hear Cassie pipe up.

"Could someone move me closer?"

Mika

I'M NOT sure what to expect when Mark wheels Cassie closer to me, and I definitely don't know how to act.

"I know I don't have the right words," she says, reaching for my hand, pressing a piece of paper to my palm and closing my fingers over it. "But what I do know is: if not for you, I wouldn't have just seen my daughter blow me a sweet kiss on my way out of her room." She shakes her head. "There aren't words to define the deep gratitude, or the deep sorrow, I feel."

"Oh, I..." is all I manage before my throat closes on whatever else I was going to say. The truth is, I'm too shocked to react, but inside my mind it's chaotic. Everything seems to be recalibrating at once.

It's not until Mark gently urges his wife it's time to get her checked out in maternity, and they leave, I realize I'm still gripping the piece of paper in my hand.

When I open it, I realize it's a long strip of graph paper. Specifically, EKG graph paper. Kelty's name and stats are printed in the top left hand corner, and her heartbeat is illustrated in the steady rhythm of lines.

Swallowing hard, I fold it back up carefully, and tuck it inside my purse for safekeeping.

"So...you and my brother."

I'd almost forgotten Ethan's still here. "Seems that way."

"Not normally a big believer in fate, or kismet—whatever it is they call it—I'm more of a pragmatist, but I gotta say this looks like more than plain coincidence."

"I know. It's a little freaky," I admit, and he bursts out laughing.

"My brother's never done things the conventional way," he shares, grinning. "Always a little wild—unhinged at times, if you ask me—always looking for something more. Not that he was stupid about it, just...restless. Even when he opened the Cooker, I always sensed it wouldn't be enough to settle him. Then Kelty came along, and she centered him. He became more focused on the here and now, instead of what all he might be missing out there." He looks over and smiles gently. "Then Mom died, which shook all of us but it hit my brother hard, and when less than a year later Kelty became ill, I worried. Up to that point, he hadn't really been tested hard in life. If a roadblock went up in one place, he'd simply moved to the next. He surprised me though. Because as much as Mark may have been the rock for all of us, Jude was the heart: the dreamer. The one who was able to keep everyone's hopes lifted. He believed so fiercely in his daughter's future, that the rest of us couldn't do more than believe right alongside him."

"I can see that. Your brother's a bit of an empath, more insightful than most. He proved that the first time he stopped me, right outside this room, in the hallway. It was only a moment during the absolute worst day of my life, but it touched me in a way that somehow stuck with me right alongside the dark memories. He makes me believe too."

Ethan chuckles. "I don't doubt it. He dreams enough for the rest of us." His expression grows serious as he leans forward. "But *you*...you may just be what grounds him."

Jude and his dad return not long after, reporting that Kelty is resting comfortably. Ethan suggests we all get some rest and invites us to stay at his place, but Jude understandably wants to stay close to the hospital. While we wait for him to check plans with Mark and Cassie in the maternity ward, I quickly call the Hilton DoubleTree next door and manage to get him a room.

My suggestion to drive back to the Cape tonight is voted down by all three men. Mark and Cassie will stay at the hospital, Jim is going with Ethan, and Jude and I are heading for the hotel. The plan is for Ethan to bring Jim back tomorrow morning, and depending how Kelty is, at least he and I will head back to the Cape.

I take a quick shower in the hotel room, while Jude orders

us some room service, which arrives just as I hear the water shut off after his turn.

"Not as good as the burgers at the Cooker," I admit around a mouthful, sitting cross-legged on the bed, wrapped only in a towel. "But it hits the spot."

"I'm surprised we're even thinking about food after today," he says almost guiltily, and I lean over to put a hand on his knee.

"I remember feeling guilty with every bite I put in my mouth," I share. "It was Sam who reminded me that I wasn't eating for me, I was eating for Jamie, so I could be strong enough for the two of us."

I see him swallow down another bite of hamburger like it was a handful of nails, but he finishes most of it.

"Why don't you check in with the nurses' station while I clean up, and we'll try to get some sleep," I suggest.

I hear him on the phone when I duck outside to leave the tray in the hallway, before quickly brushing my teeth.

"They just did her vitals and she's back asleep. Her temperature is coming down a bit and her BP and heart rate are holding strong." That makes us both smile.

I slip between the covers on the king-sized bed, ditching my towel on the ground, and wait for Jude to come out of the bathroom. The light turns off and I hear rustling as he slips between the sheets on the other side. Then a long arm shoots out, catches me around the waist, and pulls me across the mattress and into the warm curve of his body. I reach for the arm around me, take his hand, and press it against my chest as his face presses into my neck from behind.

I start drifting off when I feel his hot tears on my skin. I turn around silently, wrap him up in my limbs, and let him give all of those to me.

"I'm sorry," he finally mumbles.

"Hush," I tell him.

No words are needed.

It says enough that he trusted me to give me both his rage and his tears in a single day.

For the first time in a long while, I go to sleep feeling purposeful.

Chapter Seventeen

Jude

"SHE'S HAD A QUIET NIGHT."

The hospital is slowly coming alive when we walk up to the nurses' station in the PICU.

The alarm on my phone went off at five thirty, and we were the first to sit and scarf down some breakfast when the restaurant in the lobby opened at six.

I'd slept. I didn't think I would, but letting go of some of the bottled up emotions from the day in the safety of Mika's arms helped.

The night nurse confirms what I was told earlier when I called from the hotel to check.

"Can we see her?"

"It's family only," she says with regret, glancing at Mika who she seems to recognize.

"She *is* family," I state firmly.

She hesitates, takes a good look at us, slightly bedraggled

in yesterday's wrinkled clothes, and seems to come to a decision.

"We have a shift change coming up in fifteen minutes. You can sit with her, but if my replacement shows up, you may be asked to leave while they do their checks."

"Fair enough," I concede without argument. I'll take it.

Grabbing Mika's hand, I pull her with me down the hall to the last room. From the cart parked outside Kelty's door, I grab us masks, booties, and gloves—a prerequisite to entering because of the risk of infection—and quickly pull them on as Mika does the same.

"Morning, Princess."

Kelty's blonde hair is spread out on the pillow, her face turned to the window, but when she hears my voice she swings around to the door, her eyes bright and clear.

"Mika!"

The fact my daughter totally ignores me, as she grins at my companion, doesn't bother me at all. In fact, it warms me to know my girl is falling as hard as I am for her.

"Hey, honey." Mika's voice is hoarse when she slips past me and approaches the bed. "You're looking so much better already," she coos, gently stroking a few strands of hair away from Kelty's face.

"I didn't mean to make you worry," Kelty whispers when she notices Mika blinking furiously.

It's the second time she says something along those lines. I remember what her doctor said last night, about kids keeping concerns to themselves so as not to worry their parents, and decide it's time for a reality check.

"Princess…" Her eyes come to me. "It's our *job* to worry about you, look after you. That's what we're supposed to do. *Your* job is to let us, so we can help if needed. But when you hide stuff—important stuff, like not feeling well—you don't make it easier, you make our job harder." My heart breaks when I see her face crumple, but I have to make this clear. "Yesterday was very scary for you, but for a lot of other people as well, Kelty. People who love you. People who feel very lucky that you're doing as well as you are, but, Princess, you need to understand it could've ended much differently." I lean over the bed and brush a tear from her cheek, before putting my hand over the incision bisecting her narrow chest. "This, this precious gift you were given, you need to let us help you take care of it, baby. Do you get that?"

She nods. "I'm—"

"That better not be an apology coming out of your mouth," I threaten her. "I may have to tape it shut."

Just as easy as that, she giggles, the tears all but forgotten.

By the time the nurse comes in and sends us back to the waiting room, Kelty's dozing off again.

Mika, who's been quiet during my parental lecture, grabs my hand when we walk down the hall to the waiting room, stopping me right outside the door.

"I just want you to know you're an amazing father, a good man, and a wonderful human being."

I don't get a chance to respond—which is probably a good thing, it might not have been coherent—because in the next moment her hands are cupping my face, and she's up on her toes, kissing me stupid.

"Find yawselves a room, will ya?"

"Morning, Dad." I grin without taking my eyes off Mika.

"How's my granddaughtah?"

"Better," I share. "Fever's down. She was pretty chatty for a bit just now, before zonking out again."

He nods and grumbles something before opening the door to the waiting room, leading the way inside.

Mark joins us not long after, reporting they admitted

Cassie to Obstetrics overnight after discovering her blood pressure skyrocketing again. I admire the guy, where I'd probably be a nervous wreck; he seems calm. Only the firm statement his wife's ass will be staying in the hospital bed, even if it means handcuffing her to it, betrays the level of his concern.

We spend the morning alternating visits with Kelty while we wait for the cardiologist to check in on her.

When Dr. Cosgrove walks into the waiting room around eleven, we're all eager to hear.

"Kelty's had a good night. She's responding well to the antibiotics, and we'll be moving her to a private room in Cardiology in the next few hours."

"That's good news," Mark comments.

"It is great news," he concurs. "But she's not necessarily out of the woods yet. I'd like to see if we can adjust her medications, and then monitor her for at least a few more days before I'm comfortable discharging her."

"Whatever it takes." I shake his hand. "Thank you so much."

He nods and then his eyes drift to Mika. "Ms. Spencer. I was surprised to see you here last night. I wasn't aware you knew the family?"

"A chance meeting right here in the hospital the day of the transplant," I clarify, speaking for her. "We didn't recognize the significance of it ourselves until very recently."

"I see. I'm sure you know we have strict rules about privacy, both for the sake of the donor's family as well as the recipient's. This...is a little unconventional."

I don't even have to look at Mika to know this exchange must be extremely uncomfortable for her, but I don't get the chance to tell the man to back off.

"Ms. Spencer *is* family," Mark calmly enforces, throwing

a casual arm around her shoulders. "And as I'm sure you've noticed, Dr. Cosgrove, our family is far from conventional."

"Of course. No offense intended," he says, looking at Mika.

"None taken," she assures him, lying through her teeth.

Mika

"ARE you sure you don't mind?"

Jude's father shakes his head, waving the newspaper he found on the coffee table at my lawyer's office. "Missed my *Boston Globe*. Gives me a chance to catch up. Take yaw time."

With the immediate crisis averted, and Kelty and her mother both in the hospital, at least for a while longer, it made more sense for me to head back to Orleans. I'm better off helping out at the Cooker, doing something useful. Not much I can do here, but at least I can take a little off Jude's load.

He wasn't too enamored with my suggestion at first, but when his father said he'd tag along so he could pack a bag for everyone before driving back, he didn't resist.

I was a little embarrassed when he came down to the lobby and kissed me thoroughly—in full view of everyone—before watching us walk out to the street.

My call to Bryan's office was on the spur of the moment. I figured, while I'm here, I might as well get those papers signed before heading back. Luckily, Bryan was in the office and had everything ready, planning to call me later today.

"There you are," his voice is loud and boisterous, as he is.

I barely get a chance to turn around before he has me wrapped up in a hug.

Bryan is the only friend I retained after Emmett and I split. Unlike most of our friends, who either backed away when our marriage disintegrated, or stuck with Emmett—who was quick to garner public sympathy—Bryan had been unwavering in his support for me, even hooking me up with a good divorce lawyer when I needed one.

I worm from his arms and turn to face Jim, who is observing us closely.

"Bryan, this is Jim Parks…a friend," I add awkwardly. "Jim, meet Bryan Stewart, my lawyer and also a friend."

The two shake hands before Bryan leads me into his office.

"Don't hit me, but you look like shit," he bluntly imparts when he sits down behind his desk, gesturing to the visitor's chair.

"You would too if you had the past twenty-four hours I had," I fire back, grinning at his familiar teasing.

"Time to tell me about it?" he asks, but I shake my head.

"I will, but not now. I don't have a lot of time. I'll call you when things settle down."

"I'm holding you to that."

He hands me a pen and shoves the first of a stack of papers in front of me, and I start signing.

Twenty minutes later I follow Jim out the door, less a house, but with a whack-load more money heading to my account.

Jim doesn't say much on the drive home, but to be honest I'm grateful for the quiet, it gives me a chance to process, and there's a lot.

We make a planned detour by Mark and Cassie's place. Mark gave us his keys, so we could pick a few things up for them as well. It feels a little weird walking into a strange house and going through their drawers, but it didn't make sense for Mark to make the trek back here too, just for a few clothes and some toiletries.

I haven't even scratched the surface of what's tumbling through my mind when I pull into the parking lot next to my cottage.

Everything looks unchanged from when I first drove up here—feels like years ago—except it was just last month. Then I was a visitor, unsure of her place in the world. This time it feels familiar—the sights, the sounds, the smells—it's like coming home.

"Are ya comin' out?"

I realize Jim is already standing next to the Traverse, while I'm still deep in thought behind the wheel. I quickly turn off the engine and get out, meeting him on the other side.

"Don't go driving back right away," I say, as I hand him the keys. "I wanna make sure you have something in your stomach first. I'll get some sandwiches going while you pack a bag."

He scowls at me and walks off, mumbling something about *bossy womenfolk* under his breath.

I'm still grinning as I get to the porch steps and hear my name yelled. I swing around and see Mandy running from the restaurant toward me.

"Everything okay?" she asks, breathlessly.

"Much better. They'll keep her for another few days, but her fever is almost gone and she's starting to feel better."

"And the heart?"

I notice her generic reference, and although I understand her motivation and appreciate her sensitivity, I correct her immediately. "Kelty's heart? Steady."

She lets out a deep sigh and closes her eyes briefly. "Ah, what a relief. What are you doing back here, though?"

"Jim is picking up some clothes and stuff for him and Jude before he heads back, and I'm here to work."

"I could've managed, you know," she blusters defensively.

"Don't doubt it for a minute, but now you don't have to. Besides, I don't do well sitting around, may as well make myself useful."

I grin at her when she rolls her eyes before they land on me, squinting. "You okay?"

"Yeah. It's all good."

She scrutinizes me for a few more seconds before nodding. "Lunch is covered, so I'll see you at four," she says, starting to walk away before she adds over her shoulder, "Gives you time to wash that hospital smell off and do something about the rat's nest on your head."

I'm just stacking a few sandwiches on a plate when a knock sounds at the door.

"Door's open!"

Jim walks in and looks around, stopping on the bookcase. "That's new. Yers?"

"No. Jude picked it up at an estate sale. Have a seat. Can I get you something to drink?"

"Watah's fine."

"Coming up." I slide the plate in front of him, when he sits at the table, and go to fetch him a glass of water.

"More of my granddaughtah's?" he asks, pointing at the frames still leaning against the back of the couch.

"Actually, those are my shots. I had those made for Jude, but I haven't really had a chance to give them to him."

Jim gets up, and one by one flips the frames around. There's my shot of the heron, the one Jude liked with the water spray surrounding his head like a halo. The next one is of the whale's tail, lifting out of the water; a shot I took on our trip to Provincetown. The last two I made on that trip as well. One is a close up of Kelty's profile just as she pulls down her mask to say something to her dad, who's just outside of the frame, her eyes bright and mouth smiling wide.

Jim's eyes are a little misty as he looks up at me, before turning the last one over. That picture I took when after we got home and Jude had just laid his daughter on the couch. I caught him bending over her, kissing the tip of her nose.

I love that picture. Their faces fill the entire frame. Hers sleeping—sweet and innocent—and his dark and brooding, but infinitely tender and protective.

"He'll like those," Jim says in a gruff voice, clearly affected.

I smile my gratitude as he sits down and eats the rest of his sandwich in silence. It's not until I walk him to the door after, and watch him go down my steps that he speaks, stopping at the bottom.

"Was all kinds of wrong about ya."

Chapter Eighteen

Jude

HOSPITALS GET OLD FAST.

Especially when you're confined to a small room with a bored little girl and a grumpy old man.

I'm grateful for Mark, who'll occasionally pop in and relieve us for half an hour to grab some food, a bathroom break, or a breath of fresh air outside.

Cassie had been wheeled in here a few times as well, to sit with our daughter for a bit, before she had to get back on the monitor in her own room on the other side of the hospital. They were keeping a close eye on the baby, whose heart rate showed occasional signs of distress. She's only thirty weeks pregnant and they're doing their best to keep the baby right where it is so the lungs can mature a little more. Kelty had been a little early too, but born at thirty-six weeks, she'd been healthy and strong and was able to go home with Cassie the next day. Hopefully this baby hangs in there a little longer.

These last two nights I shared the king-sized bed at the

DoubleTree with my father, and let me tell you, it's not nearly as peaceful as it was the first night sleeping next to Mika. Dad snores, he hogs the covers, and he does not appreciate cuddling, which I discovered as he nearly shoved me out of the bed, when I apparently got a little too close in my sleep.

Still, I appreciate the hell out of him sticking it out with me. I wish it was Mika here, but if I'm honest, it gives me peace of mind she's helping Mandy and Daniel keep the restaurant going.

"Where's your dad?"

I turn to find Mark wheeling Cassie into the room.

"Gone to settle up at the hotel," I tell them. "He shouldn't be long and said he'd wait outside with the truck."

"Hey, beautiful." Cassie leans over the bed to kiss Kelty.

"Hi, Mommy, we're waiting for the nurse to come back. I get to go home."

"I heard, baby. That's great news."

"Are you going home too?" Her little face falls when her mom shakes her head.

She puts a hand on her substantial stomach. "The doctor wants to keep an eye on me so we can make sure this little pumpkin can come out healthy, sweetie."

"How long do you need to stay?"

"Well, it may be a few weeks. The longer the better it is for the baby, but I hope you'll come visit me. Dr. Cosgrove will probably want to see you again soon, so you could stop by then."

"Can we, Daddy?"

"We'll visit as often as we can, Princess," I assure her, before sticking my head out the door to see what's keeping the nurse.

There's a guy I've seen hanging around the hospital, leaning against the desk at the nurses' station. I'm about to head over there when the nurse he's talking to spots me and holds up a finger indicating she'll be right there.

Not long after she walks into the room, paperwork in her hands.

"Sorry about the wait. You ready to go?" she asks Kelty, who nods enthusiastically.

It takes another twenty minutes going over the new medication regimen and her home care instructions. It's not our first rodeo, but it's hospital procedure for them to outline every detail again before they can let us go.

When Cassie and Mark have said their goodbyes, Kelty gets dressed with the help of the nurse, while I pack up the rest of her things. Five more minutes to wait for an orderly to show up with a wheelchair and we're on our way out the door.

"Hang on," I tell them when we get to the lobby. "I'm just going to see if our ride is here." I head outside to look for Dad, who was supposed to wait for us down here.

"Mr. Parks?" I turn around at the voice and watch the guy I saw upstairs at the nurses' station earlier walk toward me.

"Yes?"

"Jude Parks?"

I don't bother answering again, but brace myself when I see him pull out some small recording device as he steps closer.

"John Meister of the *Boston Telegraph*." I narrow my eyes at the mention of the weekly local gossip rag you can pick up at the grocery store checkout. "Mr. Parks, what is your connection with Mika Spencer?"

A sudden rage boils up inside me and my hands curl into fists by my side. I'm aware of my daughter behind me in the lobby, just feet away, and squash the urge to slap the recorder he shoves in my face out of his hand. Last thing I want is for his attention to be drawn on Kelty.

I try to ignore him as he tries to block my way, pelting questions at me. Was I aware of accusations made against Ms. Spencer? What is the nature of our relationship? How did we meet? Did I know where Ms. Spencer was now?

From the corner of my eye, I see a security guard by the front doors and make my way over to him, the persistent reporter walking backward in front of me. We catch the guard's attention and he turns fully toward us, just in time to clamp a firm hand on the tabloid hack's shoulder.

"This man bothering you?"

"He is," I state firmly. "He's a reporter and I've seen him hanging around patient rooms."

The guard nods, ignoring the guy's protests as he grabs him none too friendly around his bicep, while he makes a call on the radio clipped to his shoulder.

I don't wait around to see what happens, but rush outside, where I see Dad behind the wheel of my Traverse parked down a ways. I wave him over and head straight back inside, where I just catch John Meister of the *Boston Telegraph* flanked by now two guards, being marched through a door behind the information desk.

"Ready?"

"Who was that man, Daddy?"

It's clear my daughter witnessed at least some of that confrontation, but an answer will have to wait. I'm eager to get her out of here. "Grampa's waiting outside, Princess. Let's get you in the car."

Kelty will only be distracted for so long, and by the time she's installed on the back seat, and I take Dad's place behind the wheel and start driving, she repeats her question.

"Dad? What did that man want?"

"What man?" my father wants to know, and I throw him a look before focusing on my daughter in the rearview mirror.

"Did you know Mika was sometimes on TV before she came to us?"

"Grampa told me," she says, nodding. "She was kinda famous."

"Right. Well, that man was a reporter for a newspaper asking questions about Mika, but she came to Cape Cod for some quiet time."

"Like Katy Perry hiding from the paparazzi?"

"Sort of." I chuckle and glance at my father but he doesn't look at all amused. "The guy was from the *Telegraph*. Approached me by name." I talk softly to avoid my daughter overhearing. "Seen him hanging around the hospital the past few days, but this morning he was at the nurses' station outside our room."

"Short guy, dawk messy mop that shoulda seen a barbah months ago, and one a them silly little goatee things?"

"That would be him," I confirm.

"Makes sense. Caught him in the lobby starin' when you kissed Mika the othah day."

Like a Jack-in-the-box, Kelty's head darts between the seats.

"You kissed Mika?"

Mika

I FEEL a little like the pied piper, with Nauset Beach's gull population following me around as I poke through the clumps of seaweed left in the wake of the ebbing tide.

I've only seen one fellow beachcomber this morning; an older man with a friendly dog, who enthusiastically put his wet, sandy paws all over my khaki linen pants. I didn't really care, glad for the unexpected affection, but the man had been mortified, insisting he pay for any dry-cleaning, which I refused.

The shimmer of something smooth catches my eye, and when I brush away the seaweed I see a beautiful piece of polished red glass. A rare color I know from my research, and one I don't have yet.

I quickly wipe my hands on my pants—they're dirty already—and lift my camera. I already know how I'm going to edit these shots, leaving the red of the glass intact, but draining the rest of the frame of color. I've done that with a few of the ones I found in the more common greens and blues, and the effect is quite stunning. If I group those images together, they'd make an interesting collection.

I'm building up a decent portfolio and these past few days, since the sale of the house was finalized, I've been seriously considering getting a bunch of them framed and maybe checking around if any place would be interested in displaying them. If anything, it could become a hobby that pays for itself.

When I've taken just about every composition I can think of, I carefully pick up the glass and brush the sand off. Looking at it in the palm of my hand, I notice its unique shape. It's beautiful, and I carefully wrap it in one of my lens cloths and tuck it away in my camera bag.

I start walking back to where my car is parked; while behind me the gulls descend on the pile of seaweed I left behind, scouring for anything edible I might've left behind.

To my surprise, I find the old man and his dog I'd encountered earlier sitting on the bench by the parking lot.

"I hope you don't mind," he starts. "But I was sitting here, having a little break before taking Sadie here home to her babies, when I noticed you taking pictures. My name is Giles Taylor, by the way." He holds out his hand, which I promptly shake.

"Mika Spencer."

"Nice to meet you. I realize this will sound strange—and I'd insist on paying you—but I was wondering if I could ask you to take a picture." My face must've shown my confusion because he quickly clarifies, "Of my dogs. Sadie here..." he distractedly scratches the golden retriever behind the ears, "...had a litter almost two months ago. Four of them. Unfortunately, it appears my girl has a taste for bad boys, because it's clear their father is the ugly mutt from down the street she's taken a shine too. Full breed puppies would go like hotcakes I'm told by the local shelter, but an advertisement with the description: mother full-bred golden, father unidentified neighborhood menace, apparently, doesn't make for good copy. Even when I offer them for free."

I chuckle at his description and crouch down to give slutty Sadie some loving. "So the picture...?"

"Ah, yes, the picture. I was hoping perhaps if people could see how cute they are, it might help make them more attractive. Sadly, I'm a bit of a Luddite, and don't own a camera or a mobile phone, which is why I am hoping you might be able to assist me. For a fee, of course. I just live up the road."

For a moment I contemplate the wisdom of what I'm about to do, but the man is at least eighty, if he is a day, and I could probably take him with my pinky finger if I had to.

I straighten up and sling my camera bag over my shoulder. "Then by all means, let's go take some pictures of Sadie's babies."

I finally convince Giles that Sadie can't do any harm in the back of the wagon and he gets in the passenger seat, directing me to a small, cottage-style house not that far up from the beach.

"Wait here," he says when I follow him up on the porch, where Sadie is already scratching at the door. "I have a baby gate I use to block off the porch so they can't get away."

"Perfect. I prefer using outside light to take pictures."

He sets up the little gate, disappears back inside, and comes walking out moments later with Sadie dancing around his feet, and carrying—two per arm—the most adorable puppies I've ever seen.

All four are multicolored with floppy ears and predominantly short hair, with occasional longer tufts sticking out from around their little faces. The moment he sets them on the ground, their little fat bodies toddle over and try to climb my legs. I sink down on my butt and let them clamber all over me, laughing as the little boy—the only one with blue eyes—tries to take off with one of my flip-flops.

"They are adorable," I confirm to Giles, who's taken a seat on the porch bench, wearing a benevolent smile.

"Yes. Must be Sadie's superior genes," he quips and I smile up at him.

I spend at least half an hour taking pictures while the puppies play, chatting with Giles the entire time. I know someone who would love meeting these little bundles of energy, and I ask if he would mind if I came back one day with a friend. I get the sense he doesn't get visitors a lot, if the wide smile on his face is anything to go by as he quickly agrees.

I promise I'll get the shots printed off and even offer to send a new ad with picture to the local newspaper.

"Young lady, I really appreciate your help," Giles says,

shaking my hand again when I get up, ready to head out. "But you must tell me what I owe you," he insists.

I start to climb over the baby gate when the feisty little blue-eyed pup puts his teeth in the hem of my pants. I bend down and pick him up, holding him in front of my face as he frantically wiggles his little butt, trying to lick my nose.

"They'll be old enough in a week or two, you say?"

"Ten weeks by then."

I don't really know what I'm doing, and I'm positive I've not thought this through at all, but something drives me to say, "Would you consider letting me adopt this little rascal?"

Chapter Nineteen

Jude

GOD, it feels good to be home.

I notice the parking lot is pretty full when I pull into my driveway. Looks like we have a good crowd for lunch.

"Can we go say hi, Dad?" Kelty asks from the back seat as I turn off the engine.

"You heard the nurse, Princess, we have to be extra careful for a while longer and going into a busy restaurant may not be smart. How about you have a nap, and I'll go ask everyone to pop in here to say hello if they have a chance?"

She doesn't look thrilled, but she's smart enough after these past few days not to push the issue. She walks inside under her own steam, but I carry her upstairs to her room.

"Need anything, baby?"

She rolls on her side in bed, her eyes half closed. "Is Mika your girlfriend?" she mumbles.

"What if I said she was, how would you feel about that?"

Even with her eyelids drifting shut she manages to smile wide, giving me a thumbs-up.

Dad's downstairs on the couch, with his feet on the coffee table, arms crossed over his chest, his head back, and eyes closed. A good time for me to slip out and check in at the Cooker.

Mandy comes charging from the behind the bar when I walk in and throws herself in my arms, startling not only me, but also some of the lunch crowd eating inside.

"So glad you guys are home," she mumbles before taking a step back and self-consciously brushing at the wrinkles in my shirt.

A young guy, maybe early twenties, comes out of the kitchen carrying a large tray of food. "Who's that?" I ask Mandy under my breath.

"Nick. He started yesterday." When I look at her with my eyebrows raised, she puts her hands on her hips. "It's been crazy busy, and with the weekend coming up, I needed extra hands. Figured it couldn't hurt."

"At least he looks like he knows what he's doing," I comment, watching as he serves a table of six on the patio. "Where's Mika?" I haven't seen her yet.

Mandy grins and tilts her head in the direction of my office. "She's on the phone trying to figure out where our booze is. They missed our delivery yesterday."

I'm about to head in there when the door opens and an annoyed-looking Mika walks out. She stops when she sees me and a smile breaks through.

"Five minutes, Mandy," I tell her, already moving down the hall.

Mandy's lazy, "Sure," and subsequent chuckle disappear when I back Mika into the office and kick the door shut.

"I have to check on my tables," she protests without much

conviction, as I tug her close. Her arms slip around my neck and then we're kissing.

Kissing like we're starved, like it's been months instead of a couple of days. The sweet tang of her mouth tastes like wild ocean and fresh mint. The soft curves under my hands and pressed against my body feel like home.

"God, I missed you," I mumble, as I lift my mouth from hers.

Her blue eyes sparkle with a smile as she looks up at me. "Yeah." Then her hand lifts to my cheek and she brushes a thumb under my eye. "You look tired."

"You would be too if you had to share a hotel bed with my father." She chuckles at my pained expression.

"I'll pass."

"Don't blame you. By the way, Kelty knows," I share, changing topics. "She overheard Dad and me talking on the way here." I see a flash of concern in her eyes and quickly clarify, "You and me, she likes it."

She blows out a relieved breath I can feel against my face, just a fraction away from hers. "How is she doing?"

"Napping. So is Dad."

"Happy to be home?"

"Not as happy as I am," I confess, tightening my hold on her just as the door swings open, and the new guy sticks his head in.

"Oh, sorry," he apologizes, but his eyes take us in with more curiosity than I'm comfortable with before he focuses on Mika. "Want me to serve table twenty-one? Food is ready."

"I'll be right out. Thanks, Nick."

"I don't know if I like that guy," I mumble when he shuts the door again, making her snicker.

"He's a nice guy and barely out of diapers," she says,

lifting up to press her lips against mine. "I better get out there or you're gonna get me fired."

"I might have to do it myself if I want any time with you."

"Don't you dare," she threatens, punching my shoulder. "I like working here, and love the job benefits," she teases, lifting up for another kiss before she slips from my hold.

"Mika," I call her attention when she opens the door and wait for her to turn around. "I'll be waiting for you when you get off."

The flash of heat in her eyes matches the one I feel. I may not get a whole lot of sleep tonight either.

I sit down at my desk and look over the new schedule Mandy's left there. Maybe I shouldn't complain too much about her recent hire, since it looks like it leaves Mika with a little more free time. Time I wouldn't mind spending with her.

The next hour I spend calling in the orders for the weekend I'd asked Mandy to leave on my desk. It feels good to be doing something productive, instead of hanging around the hospital.

Hanging around the hospital.

Shit. I have to remember to tell Mika about the *Telegraph* reporter seeking me out. I don't want her to be blindsided like I was if he shows up.

We should probably discuss whether or not Kelty should know where her heart came from. I'd prefer she didn't—it seems like a little too much responsibility on her little shoulders—but with the press already sniffing around, I also don't want to risk her finding out from anyone other than us.

I'm going to have to talk to Cassie and Mark too. Get their take on it.

Folding my arms behind my head, I lean back in my chair and let my gaze drift when something catches my eye. On the wall above the filing cabinet, where an old calendar hung well beyond its years, now hangs a large black and white print.

My daughter's smiling face, larger than life, with eyes so clear, I can see the reflection of the ocean in them.

Mika

"You and the boss an item?"

I'm rolling cutlery in the linen napkins for tomorrow, while Nick tops up the condiments.

"What does it look like?" I deflect, a little annoyed at the forward question.

Don't get me wrong, he seems like an overall nice guy. He's charming, has an easy way about him, and seems to fit in seamlessly, but I've known him for all of twenty-four hours. Not really at the point where we share details of our personal lives, if ever there would be such a time.

Nick shrugs, letting my sharp tone slide off his back like water. "Looks like the boss is one lucky man."

"Puleeze," I drawl mockingly. "I'm old enough to be your mother."

"Doubtful," he returns. "I'm twenty-seven." He looks like he barely celebrated his twenty-first birthday. "Besides," he continues, "you can't fault a guy trying for the hot chick who knows the difference between a linebacker and a safety."

My hand freezes midair. It's suddenly clear from the football reference, he knows who I am. My eyes squint as I look up at him. "You're from Boston."

"Quincy. Boston Sports News was one of the few presets on our TV growing up."

Ouch. Probably without realizing it, he's just aged me. I had a good twelve years in as a sports journalist with BSN before I left early last year.

"Another lifetime," I share before grabbing the bin of cutlery I've been filling, carrying it to the serving station. "Mandy," I call down the hall where I can see her sitting at Jude's desk, going over the receipts for the day. "I'm out of here."

"Four tomorrow," she calls back.

I duck my head in the kitchen, where Daniel is doing some prep work for tomorrow. "Night, Daniel."

"Night, girl."

"See ya, Nick," I say on my way out of the restaurant.

"Later, Mika."

The cottage is dark. I forgot to turn on the porch light again. I barely have the door open when I'm suddenly lifted off my feet from behind and pushed inside. The panic only lasts for the second it takes me to recognize Jude's scent, and no sooner than it takes him to kick the door shut, I turn in his arms and climb him like a tree.

"Fucking longest eight hours of my life," he growls, his hands cupping my ass as his mouth slams down on mine.

Spontaneous combustion has hands ripping at clothes, and I'm barely aware of being carried through the cottage to the bedroom. The moment my feet touch the floor, I'm tugging down my jeans and panties at once. In the span of a few seconds, we're both buck naked, panting hard as we stare at each other by just the light from the parking lot filtering in through the window.

I don't need light to see the hot desire shimmering in his eyes, or the need that has his cock hard and pulsing.

"*Mika*..." he groans when I sink to my knees in front of him, curling my hand around the silk steel of his erection. I softly blow on the crown, feeling him jerk in my hand, before sliding my lips around his girth.

There is something so powerful about feeling his body's involuntary response to my touch. This need building in him as his hand slips around the back of my head, fingers tightening in my hair, is feeding my own. I let the taste of him imprint itself on my senses as I work his length, trying to take in as much as I can. When I slip a hand around his heavy sac, tugging slightly as I extend a finger to rub his taint, he hisses sharply.

"Babe, you do that I'm gonna blow and I want to be inside you when I do." He grabs me under my arms, ignoring my sounds of protest, and pulls me to my feet. "That felt way too good," he mumbles, pressing his lips to mine as he backs up to the bed, falling back and pulling me down with him. "If I didn't feel like I need to be inside you now," he says through grinding teeth as he moves my legs so I'm braced with a knee on either side of his hips. "I'd love to let you explore every fucking inch of my body, and I'd do the same to you." His hands are on my hips, rocking me along his hard length. "Fuck, you're so wet. Feel what you do to me?" His hips flex up, grinding his cock against my clit, and I moan as my head falls back. "Beautiful. You're so goddamn beautiful it hurts." He surges upright, taking me with him, and buries his face between my breasts. "Jesus, you smell good. Let me inside, baby."

His breath is choppy as I lift my hips under his firm guidance and slide myself slowly down on his cock.

"*Jude*..." I cry out when I feel the sharp sting of his teeth on the swell of my breast. He soothes the bite with his tongue, before drawing my nipple deep into the heat of his mouth.

Glorious.

The way he heats me inside and out, I feel like I've been sparked to life. Every hair on my skin stands on end, charged by his touch as his rough palms slide over my body with an urgent reverence. His own muscles ripple when I restlessly stroke his shoulders and back, memorizing every ridge and valley, as I grind myself down on his length.

Time doesn't exist as our bodies take what they need from each other: skin sliding over skin, slick with the heat we generate.

"ARE YOU HUNGRY?"

I chuckle at the question. So like a guy.

I was almost asleep, snuggled with my cheek to his chest, and leg thrown over his, as his fingers draw circles on my hip.

"I guess I could eat something. Let me make us a sandwich," I offer, getting ready to roll out of bed.

"I'll go," he says firmly.

Five minutes later, he's back with a couple of waters from the fridge and a stack of sandwiches on a plate.

"You don't have any beer," he mumbles through his first bite, settling back against the headboard.

"I don't drink much anymore. I did too much of that for a while." I take a quick sip of my water and glance at him from under my lashes.

"Oh?" He tries hard not to be nosy, but it's something I've decided to be open about anyway.

"Drinking got me into trouble," I confess. "Actually, drinking and sedatives got me into trouble." He swallows hard before he puts his sandwich down and takes a sip of water himself, steeling himself for what I'm sure he knows is coming. "I was looking for a way to feel numb. Both worked, but together they worked a little too well." I look down at my hands. "If I'm perfectly honest, I don't even know if it was a mistake. Sam found me unresponsive, called an ambulance. I was in an inpatient treatment facility for a while. At my own request," I add. "When I saw how I'd traumatized my best friend, I owed it to her...heck, I owed it to Jamie not to give up."

"You don't have to tell me this," he says softly, stroking the back of his fingers down my cheek, and I close my eyes at the comfort of such a simple touch.

"I do," I disagree. "The way our lives are connected, I want...no, I *need* for you to know everything there is to know. I can't afford to risk losing you, what we have, because it's almost inevitable some of it will bubble to the surface eventually, especially when the press gets involved."

I feel more than see the tension in him, and I realize I hadn't even considered the possibility he might have second thoughts.

"The press?" The angry growl is clearly not at me, but because of me. There's a vast difference.

"They were still hovering. It made for juicy fodder for a day or two on the pages of the *Boston Telegraph*. They're hardly worth the title of newspaper."

I try to brush it off, but Jude is having none of it. He sets the plate aside and leans over, cupping my face in his hands. "Fuck, baby. I'm so sorry. Christ, I hate to tell you this, but it doesn't look like they're done yet."

I'm confused. "What do you mean?"

"The *Telegraph*. Some guy by the name of John Meister shoved a recorder in my face just as we were leaving the hospital."

The implications rush at me all at once, making my stomach turn.

Chapter Twenty

Jude

"CASSIE OKAY?"

I watch Mika walking hand in hand with my daughter, down the beach to the water's edge, as I stop to take Mark's call.

It's a cloudy Monday morning and Nauset Beach has been virtually deserted since we got here. I've been mostly following those two around, listening with half an ear to their exchanges. All photography slang, I'm surprised to find my daughter already has a working understanding of. Mika has taught her a thing or two already. I'm clearly not needed here, but Kelty insisted I come.

She's been pretty much over the moon with Mika's changed status in our lives and seems determined to force us together. Not that it's necessary; aside from working, we've also been spending most of our time off in each other's company this past weekend. Including our nights in the cottage.

I've set my alarm every morning, so I could be back at the house before Kelty woke up, but this morning I was a little distracted after it went off and Kelty was already sitting on the steps with her camera. I'd given the green light for her to resume her morning adventures with Mika, and clearly my daughter was eager. That's when she cornered me into coming.

Before the weekend, I'd already warned both Cassie and Mark about the reporter, in case he showed up in the maternity ward, and we talked about the risk of Kelty finding out about the origin of her heart. We agreed we should jointly tell her. It was Mika who had some valid concerns around Kelty perhaps feeling guilty. Something like survivor's guilt. It makes sense, as I told her, but it doesn't negate the fact it's safer she finds out from us. Any resulting guilt we can deal with. All of us.

"Cassie's fine," Mark says. "I know you don't bother much with TV or the internet, but you may want to check out today's *Boston Telegraph*. I happened to see a copy lying in the hospital cafeteria this morning. I started flipping through, and let me just tell you, I didn't need to see even the blurred out version of your ass before having my coffee."

"What?"

"There's a picture of you, and Mika from what I can see, on page three of the *Telegraph*. Short little story, but pretty suggestive."

"You have got to be shitting me."

"Nope. I wish I were, I'm scarred for life."

"Fuck!"

Apparently I'm a little too loud when Mika swings around and looks at me with concern. I quickly give her a thumbs-up before I turn away.

"Are you still coming in tomorrow after Kelty's appointment?"

"Abso-*fucking*-lutely. Especially after this."

My clumsy thumbs keep messing up as I try to look up the *Telegraph's* website on my phone after he hangs up.

"Son of a bitch…" I mutter when page three of the gossip rag appears on my screen.

The picture is taken through the bedroom window at the cottage. It shows me mostly from the back, my ass covered by a blurry circle, but what kills me is it shows Mika face on. She's clearly on her knees in front of me, her face lifted up, and even with the mattress covering her from the shoulders down at this angle, the intent is clear.

"Everything okay?" I hear Mika right behind me. I didn't even notice her walking up. My eyes find Kelty a little down the beach, aiming her camera at something in the distance.

I press the screen of my phone to my chest as I turn around.

"No."

Shock registers on her face at my blunt answer, but no pretty packaging is going to make this any easier. Ripping off the Band-Aid is the only way to go.

"The *Telegraph* has pictures of us in today's edition. Mark happened to flip through a copy in the hospital and called right away."

"Pictures?"

"Yeah, baby. Brace, because it ain't pretty."

I hand her my phone and watch as her teeth dig into her bottom lip and a deep red blush crawls up her neck.

I'm not sure what I expected—tears maybe—but certainly not the steel determination in those blue eyes when she lifts them to me.

"Right. Go get Kelty, Jude," she orders me with an edge

that tells me not to poke the bear. "I have a newspaper to sue and you have an asshole to fire."

"What asshole are you talking about?"

"Who do you think?" she snaps and I see she's barely hanging on. "That fucking little pervert, Nick."

"Kelty!" I immediately belt out. "We've gotta go."

My daughter is still pouting in the back seat when we get home, even with the promise of a sundae for lunch.

"Hang on so I can drop her off with Dad," I tell Mika, who's already half out the door.

"Let me do this, please?" she pleads, her eyes echoing her words. "For once I'd like to stand up for myself."

It goes against the grain to let her do the dirty work, but I nod anyway. I'll do anything for her; even swallow my need to jump to her protection. "I won't be far behind you, though," I call out as she's already marching over to the restaurant.

Mika

OH, I'm fuming.

Mortified, but fuming.

Aside from feeling violated with the publication of photos of what was such a profound and intimate moment, I am beyond livid that they dare drag a good decent man and father through the mud with me.

I may not have had it in me to fight when it was just my reputation getting trashed, but I will not stand by when they go after Jude, or God forbid, Kelty.

"You!" I yell, as I slam through the doors.

Nick is standing beside Mandy, who looks at me like I've grown horns. I probably have. "What on earth, Mika?"

"Not you. Him." I reach out, grab Nick by the wrist and pull him down the hallway to Jude's office. He doesn't resist.

"Look, it's just business," he has the gall to say when I drop his arm and shut the door on a curious Mandy.

"You call it just business?" I hiss, walking over to the filing cabinet and pointing at the close-up of Kelty I hung there for Jude. Behind a blank-looking Nick the door opens and Jude slips in, but he stays leaning against the doorframe, his arms crossed over his chest. "It's about this little girl's life, you miserable scum-sucking piece of shit! I'm fair game, but this beautiful little girl, who's been through hell and back this past year, does not deserve what you've set in motion." I hate the tears that are burning tracks down my cheeks and I wipe at them impatiently. "This is business to you? Let's call law enforcement right now and see what they think of your kind of business. Misrepresenting yourself, spying on people, taking their picture and publishing them with some sensationalized version of the truth. What is wrong with you?"

The mention of the cops seems to be the only thing that elicits any kind of reaction from him. "Look, I had nothing to do with that article, I just do what I'm told, and I was told to take some pictures."

I look over at Jude, who's walked over to the desk and is talking on the phone. To the cops, I hope. I turn back to Nick. "Those were not just some pictures and you know it. Still, you got them, so what the hell are you still doing here?" My eyes narrow on him when he tries to look away, clearly uncomfortable now. "Nick—is that even your name? Nick?" His lips press together and he doesn't say anything more, but starts slowly backing up. "You have more pictures, don't you?"

I move to close the distance but he's faster and darts out the door, only to be shoved right back inside by a looming Daniel, who apparently was right outside. The much bigger man keeps pushing him until the backs of his knees hit a chair and he plops down.

"Hey, you can't manhandle me. I'll file charges."

Daniel plants his hands on the chair railings, down to where he's almost nose to nose with Nick, and his voice is a deep rumble. "Try."

"Vern'll be here in a few," Jude says, walking up and throwing an arm around my shoulders.

"He's gotta have more pictures," I tell him, feeling like a large fist is squeezing my lungs.

"Vern will take care of it."

I shake my head, trying to ward off the panic. What if he took pictures of Kelty? "But I know how these guys work. He...he..."

The words get stuck in my throat and suddenly Jude is right there in my face, holding it between his hands. "Mika, baby...breathe."

"He took our picture. He was *watching* us. My face...it's all over Boston...Oh my God."

I find myself pressed to his chest, one of his hands firmly holding me there as I proceed to lose it on him.

I keep my face pressed in his shirt, trying to calm my breathing when I register someone else coming in.

"Boss, Vern's here," I hear Mandy announce.

"Send him in." Then I hear his voice next to my ear. "I'm gonna let you go, okay?"

I nod my head against his chest before lifting it away. "I'm sorry," I mumble, peeking up at him.

He grins down at me. "Don't apologize. That was the best

tongue lashing I've ever been witness to, and well worth the wet shirt."

Ten minutes later, Nicholas Castleton—the name Jude's cop friend found on the driver's license in his wallet—is escorted out of the restaurant in handcuffs by an officer.

"What's going to happen to those pictures?" I ask Vern, a portly man in his fifties and a sergeant with the Orleans PD, pointing at Nick's iPhone in his hand.

"You tell me, do you want to press charges?" he counters with his own question, glancing at Jude who waits for me to answer.

"Yes."

I'm done, and I want this over with.

"Then these will have to be presented to the prosecutor's office as part of the evidence. There are a few charges we can slap on him, but it's up to the prosecutor to decide."

The thought of other people looking at those pictures on his phone gives me the shivers, even though at least one of them has already been published for all to see.

"I suggest you talk to a lawyer, get some advice on how to best proceed from here, because you and I both know taking this man into custody does not solve your problem."

"I know."

When Vern says his goodbyes, and Jude and I are the only ones left in his office, he turns to me.

"I'm closing the restaurant tomorrow."

"What? Why?"

"Because I have a feeling, before long, others may show up here and we need to do some damage control first."

"How do you propose to do that?"

"Well…" he rounds the desk, sits on the edge, and pulls me between his legs. "First thing tomorrow we find us a lawyer, then we drive in to Boston for Kelty's appointment, and finally we sit down with Cassie and Mark—maybe we can get Dr. Cosgrove to join—and talk to Kelty. After that I propose we pick a paper or a news station that you think would have the most impact, and offer them an exclusive on our story."

I stiffen in his hold. "What?"

"Listen, Cassie and Mark need to be in agreement, but the only way to stop this is to spoil the mystery. You pick one of the channels or papers, use your connections, and see who's interested in an exclusive."

I clap my hands on his cheeks and press my lips to his. "That might just work."

He grins at that. "Added benefit is that you finally get a chance to stick it your asshole ex."

"You just might be brilliant," I tell him with a smile.

"Might be?"

Chapter Twenty-One

Jude

"WHAT ARE YOU DOING?"

Walking into the bedroom, I find Mika on her knees beside the bed, pulling something from underneath.

I ended up sleeping in my own bed last night. It had been late after we'd closed the restaurant down, and I didn't want to oversleep and have Kelty waking up to me gone again. Actually, it had been Mika who had to kick me out, when a goodnight kiss—after I walked her to the cottage—led to a pretty heated make out session just inside her door.

Kelty is eating her breakfast at home, and I wanted to give Mika a heads-up we'll be leaving soon. Okay, fine, and maybe grab the small window of opportunity to kiss her properly, which is not necessarily appropriate in front of my daughter.

Her coffee cup was sitting on the porch railing, and her front door was open, so I walked in.

"Oh, you startled me," she says, rubbing a spot on her head where she banged it on the bed frame.

"Need some help?" I motion to the stack of large frames on the floor at her knees.

"Yes. No, these were supposed to be a surprise your father is helping with."

"Dad?"

He'd been eager to find out why the hell there'd been two patrol cars pulling in the parking lot, but had the presence of mind to keep Kelty distracted. While Mika explained the lay of the land to the full-time staff, I took the opportunity to pop over and check on my daughter. I took Dad aside and filled him in. He offered to stay behind today to keep an eye on the place. Just in case of unwanted visitors.

"Yes." She blows a stray lock of hair from her face, as she grabs onto the edge of the mattress and pulls herself to her feet. "He was going to hang these for me. Have it all done by the time we get back."

One by one she picks up the frames, propping them up side by side against the wall underneath the window. I recognize some of the photos, but others are new. Eight altogether, not counting the one still upside down by her feet.

"Those are amazing," I tell her truthfully.

They are. Predominantly black and white, with one single-colored focus. The tail of a whale, with the only color the lighthouse in the background. A piece of red sea glass peeking out from underneath seaweed. The green blistering paint on the stern of the old fishing boat down by the water, just visible in the frame featuring the white heron. All of them portraying slices of life on the Cape. Every one of them stunning.

"You're father was going to hang those in the restaurant. A little presumptuous on my part, I guess—and we could've easily taken them down again—but I hoped maybe you'd like them."

I close the distance and tag her around the neck, pulling her into a bruising kiss.

"Love them." Her smile is small, but it lights up her face. "What about that one?" I point at the one frame left upside down on the floor.

"Your dad says that should go in your bedroom."

My imagination momentarily spins out of control with the possibilities, but then I realize since Dad's seen it, it's unlikely to be a sexy boudoir shot or nude selfie of Mika.

She bends down and lifts the last frame, laying it right side up on the bed.

It's not what I expected. The close-up of Kelty's sleeping face as I kiss her is much more.

I try to breathe through the sting in my nose as I nod my head.

"Definitely my bedroom," I manage in a hoarse voice.

I LOOK OVER AT MIKA, who is wearing an indulgent smile on her face, as my daughter fills the silence with her chatter. She catches me looking and gives my hand she's been holding, since we started driving, a squeeze.

"So can I, Dad?"

"Sorry, Princess, can you what?"

"Buy the baby a stuffed animal from the hospital store," she clarifies, a tad irritated that I've not paid attention.

"The baby isn't here yet, though."

"I know," she singsongs. "But in case the baby comes and I'm not around."

Beside me Mika stifles a chuckle, as I pull into the parking garage.

"Tell you what. We're a little early for our appointment with Dr. Cosgrove, and I have a small errand to run first, but maybe Mika wouldn't mind helping you pick something out?"

An enthusiastic "Yesss" sounds from the back seat, as Mika shoots me a questioning glance. I give her what I hope is a reassuring smile.

When we walk into the lobby, I watch the two go into the small gift shop before I make a beeline for the cardiology department. It's a crapshoot, I'm not even sure she is working right now, but I really want to have a chat with the nurse I saw talking with John Meister last week.

I'm in luck. Although, I'm not too sure the woman feels the same way when she looks up from the chart she's studying and sees me coming toward her. A red flush stains her cheeks as her eyes dart around, probably looking for an escape.

"Hi. I'm sure you remember me?" She's clearly uncomfortable, but I don't give a flying fuck. "You know I saw you talking to that reporter, John Meister. Just as I'm sure you've seen what he ended up printing in that piece of shit gossip rag of his." The color on her face deepens as she averts her eyes. "I also know that was probably not the first time you spoke with him, but what I don't get is why? Did he offer you money? Did you get paid to share my little girl's confidential medical information?"

Her mouth opens and closes a few times before she manages to say, "I hit on some hard times. I...John said it was background for a human interest story."

"And you believed him?" I can tell from her reaction to my question she hadn't bought his line, but went along anyway. "Never mind answering, I can read it on your face." I flip around the phone I've been holding in my hand to show her I've recorded our conversation. "I don't care what your reasons are to be honest—there isn't a single good one I can think of to justify throwing a ten-year-old girl under the bus. I will hand this over to hospital administration and let them take care of you."

Feeling a smidge better, I head over to Dr. Cosgrove's office, where I told Mika and Kelty I'd meet them.

Mika

NERVES HAVE my stomach doing backflips and I can't stop glancing around me. With my kind of luck, someone who's read the article will recognize me and blurt out something in front of Kelty before we've had a chance to talk to her.

"Do you think the baby'll like this one?" She holds up a cute little pink bunny.

"What's not to like? How about this one?" I point at a slightly more non-gender-specific stuffed puppy.

The thing reminds me of the little blue-eyed real pup I haven't even mentioned to Jude yet. The quiet life I was expecting to find on the Cape has been anything but. More like an emotional spin cycle. I don't know if he has a strict no-pet policy, or whether either he or Kelty have allergies. My on-the-spot decision to adopt the pup didn't include any of those considerations. I make a mental note to address that one as soon as possible as well, since I promised Giles I'd pick Rascal up a week from today.

"I love puppies," Kelty mumbles, as she grabs the stuffed

animal and tucks it under her chin, while I perform an inner
fist pump. "Dad said when I'm old enough to look after it.

Good. Not averse to dogs and clearly no allergies.

"That makes sense. I remember we had a dog growing up.
My mom would feed it, but I had to walk it. I didn't always
enjoy that part," I share, remembering Toby, our black and
white Jack Russell terrier, who'd always bark at other dogs
and pull on the leash.

She decides on the puppy for the baby, and I pick up a
kid's puzzle book for Kelty, in case she gets bored, and a few
magazines and a lavender-scented hand cream for Cassie.

Jude's already waiting outside Dr. Cosgrove's office,
smiling when we walk in. Whatever he needed to take care
of, it left him in a good mood.

The wait isn't very long, and neither is Kelty's appointment, but I still manage to build up an army of anxious
butterflies in my stomach by the time they walk out of the
office.

"Ms. Spencer," Dr. Cosgrove offers me his hand.

"Mika, please."

"Certainly." He smiles and gestures down the hall. "Shall
we go then?"

Kelty slips her hand in mine as we lead the way. I hang
onto that token of affection for dear life, not sure what will
happen after she finds out.

———

"WE HAVE SOMETHING TO TELL YOU."

Cassie doesn't hesitate to set the wheels in motion after
greetings are exchanged. Since I'm fighting down my embar-
rassment and using my professional on-camera face to hide
my discomfort, I'd rather get it over with.

"Is it bad news?" Kelty looks around the room at everyone, and I realize how this must look to her.

"No," I rush to tell her before anyone else has the chance. "It isn't." I catch Jude's encouraging nod to go ahead and I take a deep breath. "I had a son. Jamie. He was thirteen."

"Did he die?" she asks with the blunt honesty of a wide-eyed, ten-year-old kid.

"Yes," I promptly respond, matching her bluntness as I feel the comfort of Jude's hand on my shoulder.

"I'm sorry." Her earnest little voice almost has me lose it, but I shore myself up.

"I am too. Jamie was a great kid and I miss him a lot, but what has made it easier is knowing he was able to help quite a few people get better. Someone was almost blind, but Jamie's corneas helped them see again. Other people received his kidneys, his liver…"

"His heart?" Her little voice is a squeak as she astutely connects the dots. Smart as a whip.

"Yes, Princess," Jude says from behind me. "Your heart was Jamie's first."

Her tear-filled eyes dart around the room, looking for confirmation in every face before she finally lands on mine.

"Is that why you like me so much?"

The air is pressed from my lungs, and for what feels like the longest time, I can't seem to take my next breath.

"No," I finally manage to say in a firm enough voice. "That's not why. I'd been really sad for a long time when I came to Cape Cod. I was hoping maybe I could learn to be happy again. Then I woke up one morning and found this amazing little person on my steps. She taught me all about the great white heron, and helped me see the beautiful world around us I'd been blind to for a while." I lean over and she lets me take her hand. "That, Kelty Parks, is why I like you so much. I didn't even know about your heart until later."

"You didn't?"

"I had no idea. I just knew this little girl who had me look forward to her visits. Then I recognized your father and I knew right away."

"You're not mad at me?"

I have to close my eyes for a moment at the tearful worry in her crystal-blue eyes.

"Not at all. Finding out Jamie's heart is what keeps you alive—this amazing girl I've come to care about a great deal —is the best gift ever. You're Jamie's very special last gift to me." I can't hold back the tears anymore and lower my head.

"And to me." Jude's voice is rough behind me.

"To me as well," Cassie sniffles.

"Count me in," Mark adds, not unaffected.

I lift my head to find Kelty's eyes on me.

"Do you have a picture?" she asks.

"I do."

"Can I have one?"

"Absolutely."

She nods thoughtfully.

"I want to hang it in my room so I won't forget."

Chapter Twenty-Two

Jude

"BUT MIKA, *why didn't you publicly defend yourself before?"*

"Because if it became known that Jamie's organs were donated, it's possible I could've exposed the donor recipients and their families to the dogged pursuit I've been victim to. I had no desire to risk compromising the basic right to privacy of innocent families. As the recent publication by John Meister of the Boston Telegraph proves, some members of our fine profession stop at nothing."

"Ah, yes. Would you be surprised if I told you John Meister and Emmett Ainsworth, your ex-husband, were fraternity brothers in college?"

"I didn't meet Emmett until a few years after he'd graduated, so I wouldn't know. However, it doesn't surprise me, neither man is blessed with a functioning moral compass."

. . .

"AGAIN?"

I grin when Mika stops in the doorway of her bedroom, a hand on her hip. "It's my favorite part." I must've replayed this clip ten times in the past couple of days.

On the advice of a lawyer Mika contacted—and to try and keep the focus off Kelty—she insisted doing the interview alone. It was broadcast by two major area radio stations and published in print in the biggest Boston newspaper on Wednesday.

During the interview, Mika consistently avoided naming names and instead stuck to the general term of organ recipient families. The only admission she made was that she'd become friendly with one of the families. Although I don't harbor any illusions it'll be enough to keep the occasional die-hard vulture off our property, I'm comfortable we won't be overrun by the press.

"Come here."

She raises an eyebrow and tilts her head, but slowly approaches until I can grab her hips and pull her between my legs. Her hands land on my shoulders when I slide mine up her sides. "Jude…"

"Yeah, baby," I mumble, nuzzling her breasts.

"We don't have time," she warns, and I press my forehead to her sternum. "We'll spoil the surprise if we don't get going now."

Dad's taken Kelty to meet up with Mark who is at their place in Chatham, checking on the house and picking up mail. In the meantime, Mika and I are supposed to be picking up a puppy.

It hadn't taken her long to convince me. Heck, the woman could get me to agree to anything as long as it made her happy. The moment she mentioned the puppy she wanted to get, my wishful mind translated that into a sign she was maybe considering staying. Here in Orleans.

We've been so busy dealing with a new crisis almost daily; we haven't really discussed any future. A future I desperately want with Mika. She fits here—in Orleans, in the restaurant, in our lives—heck, this woman fits my heart.

I lift my head and look up at her. "Let's get you your puppy," I concede, seeing the blush of excitement on her cheeks.

"His name is Rascal," she announces, a smile playing on her lips as I get behind the wheel. "He's the only one in the litter with blue eyes."

She already mentioned this when she told me about meeting old Giles Taylor on the beach, a couple of weeks ago, and getting snared into taking pictures for his ad. The guy is a loner, mostly. Comes into the Cooker from time to time, usually sits by himself at the bar, chatting with whoever is behind it.

"You know Kelty's gonna fall in love with that dog, right?"

"Yeah," she says with a big grin not quite getting my point.

"Hmmm, it would be hard for her to let him go." I glance over and catch her looking at me confused. "Should you decide to leave," I clarify, blowing out a deep breath.

"Leave? Why would I want to leave?"

"Well, we haven't really talked about anything beyond the summer."

"That's true, I just thought…" I don't like the hesitation I hear in her voice.

"Thought what?" Another quick glance shows her biting her lip, her eyes on the road ahead.

"I kinda assumed I'd be here, stay here, but if you…"

I swing the Traverse into the parking lot of the Stop & Shop and throw it in park, turning in my seat. "I want you to stay," I tell her firmly, lifting my hand to her face. "Already I can't remember what things were like before you got here, and I know they'll never be the same—fuck, I'll never be the same—if you were to leave. But, Mika, you're the only one who can make that call. You told me you came here to look for a purpose, and I guess the question is, have you found it? Your purpose?"

"I love it here." She lifts her hand to cover mine. "Love the pace, the cove, the beach, the people. I love who I am here. I love waking up early and watching the heron stalking the water's edge, looking for food. I love that sometimes Kelty's singsong voice is the first thing I hear. I *love* your beautiful, bright little girl. I even love your grumpy father, though he didn't care for me much at first. And, Jude…" She leans forward, pressing her forehead to mine. "…I love *you.*"

Fuck me.

A sigh escapes her lips right before I claim her mouth. I'm at a loss for words, and try to put all I'm feeling into the kiss. It's not enough, and I desperately fumble to release her seat belt, and haul her over the center console onto my lap. My hands slide under her shirt to the smooth skin of her back as she moans into my mouth.

She's staying.

I feel like my chest might burst when her fingers twist in my hair and she presses herself into me, as hungry as I am for full body contact.

The honking of a car horn functions like a freezing cold shower, shocking us apart, both gasping for air. She scrambles over the console, settling in her own seat, looking scrumptiously disheveled, wearing a bright blush high on her cheeks.

"Mika," I call her attention and wait for her blue eyes to meet mine. "In case I wasn't clear: I'm fucking over the moon you feel that way, because, baby…" I grab her hand and press the palm against my chest. "…you've been in here for a while."

Mika

I CAN'T STOP SMILING.

All the way home I hold Rascal in my lap, and he's making sure to let me know how happy he is. His little body worms and wiggles on my lap with his attempts to lick me.

"I know how he feels," Jude comments dryly, giving me the side-eye. "Looks like I'll have some competition for your affection."

I grin over at him, realizing it's been a long time since I've felt this kind of simple happiness. Even just a few months ago, I would've felt guilty even smiling. Don't get me wrong, I grieve for my son every day—feel that hole in my heart his loss left me with in a way I don't think can ever be filled—but I can't help feel that somehow he'd be happy for me. That maybe he would want me right here, where I can be witness every day to the legacy he left behind. I'd like to imagine perhaps he had a hand in guiding me to this place, to these people, who in a short time have become so important to me.

"What's wrong?" Jude sounds concerned.

"Nothing," I smile through the tears I realize are trailing down my face. "I'm happy, which makes me a little sad."

He reaches for my hand and gently kisses the back of it. "I get that."

I believe he does.

"OH MY GOD! A PUPPY!"

Barely through my door, Kelty drops down on her knees.

We managed to sneak Rascal in when we saw Jim and his granddaughter were already home as we drove up. Jude had gone in his house to distract her, while I beelined it for the cottage. I would've brought him into the main house, but Jude was afraid his daughter would assume Rascal was for her instead of my dog.

I just smiled and did what he asked. He'd find out soon enough I never intended Rascal to be only mine.

"What's his name?" she asks, barely keeping herself upright as the pup crawls all over her.

"Rascal."

"You're so beautiful," she coos, making the dog wag his little tail even harder.

I grin over her head at Jude, who is rolling his eyes to the ceiling.

"Ugly mutt, if ya'ask me," Jim, who followed them over, points out.

"Is not!" Kelty immediately protests, but Jim is right: aside from those bright blue eyes, Rascal isn't exactly blessed in the looks department.

Adorable maybe, cute definitely, but beautiful is not exactly accurate. Although an argument can be made that beauty is in the eye of the beholder, and the way Kelty looks at the pup, it's clear right now he's beautiful to her.

"Can he sleep with me?"

"He's Mika's dog, though, Princess," her dad reminds her gently.

"I actually thought we might be able to share him," I suggest, almost bursting out laughing when I see Jude's panicked eyes flash to me. "But for now, we'll keep him here with me. He still has so much to learn, he needs to be potty-trained. For the next little while, I'm sure he'll need to be taken out a few times during the night, and you know you need your rest. When he's a little older, though, and knows how to sleep through until morning, maybe he can come for a sleepover with you."

"Hope the mutt's had his shots," Jim grumbles, turning on his heel and walking out the door.

"Your dad doesn't seem too pleased," I mutter, when Jude steps behind me and hooks an arm around my middle, pulling my back against his front.

"Don't care about Dad," he says softly, as we watch Kelty roll on the ground, giggling when Rascal won't stop licking her. "But you didn't tell me we'd be sharing a bed with the dog."

"Can't let him lick you, honey," I quickly tell Kelty, ignoring Jude for now. "Even wearing your mask. It's possible to catch things from a dog too, especially when your immune system is compromised. You'll also have to make sure to wash your hands real well after you play with him."

"Are you ignoring me?" Jude mumbles, his lips against my ear.

"I'm setting priorities," I tease him, turning in his arms and tilting my head back. "And I'm sorry, but you weren't it."

"Ouch, woman. Way to put a guy in his place. Not only do I play second fiddle to my daughter, but to her dog as well. You're lucky I love you."

I am—both loved and lucky—I can read it in his deep brown eyes.

"I am," I confirm before adding, "but I thought Rascal was supposed to be *my* dog?"

He tugs my head back and kisses me sweetly.

"Same difference," he whispers against my smiling lips when Kelty pipes up.

"Ewww, you guys."

Chapter Twenty-Three

Jude

"Good to have you back."

I fold Trisha in a bear hug, which she only allows for a second before virtually shoving me off. She's always been bristly at best. Tough, opinionated, and direct, which is oddly what makes her fit in so well with the rest of the crew. Mandy is our mother hen, even though she's younger than most of us, with the exception of the part-time summer help and Penny, who is our resident innocent.

Daniel is the tease, Melissa is the clear head, and I'm the dreamer.

Mika—with her quiet strength—has become an integral part of the team over the summer, slipping from one role to the other, depending on the circumstances. She's the adaptable one.

"She still here?" Trisha curtly points out as Mika walks in from the kitchen.

"To stay," I inform her, which appears to surprise her.

"No shit," she mumbles, looking at me curiously. "It's like that, is it?"

"It absolutely is."

"Well, dayum. Didn't think she had it in her," she shares just as Mika walks up.

"Good to see you, Trisha. Who didn't have it in her?" Her smile is friendly enough but her eyes are sharp.

Trisha being Trisha, she doesn't hesitate to give her a straight answer. "You. Thought you'd'a been gone by now. Back to your fancy life in Boston. Coulda knocked me down with a feather, seeing you still hangin' around."

"Nothing to go back to. I'm not planning on going anywhere."

It's a challenge if I ever heard one, especially when she slips her arm through mine, facing off with Trisha. With them on either side of me, I'm starting to feel like the monkey in the middle, and wonder if maybe I should duck.

Trisha surprises me when she starts to chuckle. "There's the fire. Maybe I could learn to like her after all," she addresses me as if Mika isn't standing right beside me.

"I'm thinking that'd probably be a good thing, seeing as she sleeps with your boss."

"Jude!" Mika pokes a disgruntled finger between my ribs, and when Trisha laughs, she pokes the same finger at her. "And don't you encourage him," she adds before snagging her tray and marching out to the patio.

"She'll do."

***

"Cove Side Cooker."

"Ya left yaw phone."

"Dad? What's up?"

I tilt my chair back so I can see the front of my house through the window.

"Mawk called. It's time."

I shoot up so fast my chair slams into the wall.

"Cassie?"

"Sounds like. Give him a call."

Cassie had a few scares before, but each time they were able to slow down her contractions. Now at thirty-seven weeks, I guess the baby is ready.

I'm already walking out of the office when Mark picks up the phone.

"For real this time?"

"You wouldn't ask me that if you saw the claw marks on my arms," he shoots back, sounding a little rattled, something I've not heard before from the man. I guess it's not every day you become a father.

"We're on our way."

"That'd be good. This lasts much longer, and I may need a spare set of arms while these are stitched up." I can hear Cassie cursing at him in the background and chuckle as I hang up.

All I have to do is meet her eyes across the restaurant and it's as if she can read them like a book. She doesn't even hesitate as she stalks over.

"It's time?"

"Apparently."

"Go on then," she urges, as she starts pushing me to the door. "You don't want Kelty to miss it."

I grab her hand when she threatens another shove to my shoulder. "I want you to come with me."

"I can't. The restaurant," she mutters as her eyes dart around.

"Trish is here, they can handle it," I insist when I see the veiled excitement in her eyes.

"Cassie may not want me there."

"You should know by now that's not how it works. Cassie is all about family, and fucked up as it may seem to an outsider, family is what you and I are to her."

Her eyes shimmer but her lips pull into a smile. "Let's go then."

"Mandy!" I call out. "It's time, we're outta here."

"We've got it, Boss. Don't worry about Rascal; I'll look after him. Good luck!"

It still takes us half an hour before we're all piled in my truck heading for Boston. We all had to pack a quick bag in case we'd be staying the night, and Mika almost forgot her camera.

Dad's in front with me, and Mika sits beside Kelty in the back. My little girl is almost vibrating she's so excited.

Turns out an hour and a half is a long time to be confined in the car with a kid hopped up on adrenaline. Feels like we've gone over every possible name for a boy, or a girl, by the time I park the truck. The girl's almost in meltdown mode when I insist she wear her mask before getting out, but a sharp look and admonishing, "Kelty," from her grampa averts a crisis.

"You guys wait here, I'll go see where they are." I point at the waiting room before heading over to the nurses' station.

"Mr. Sommers already alerted us you'd be coming. I'll tell him you're here."

I remember this from last time, the sense of wonder that permeates labor and delivery, knowing that behind each one of these doors a new life is about to start. A new family is born.

"Jude." I hear my name and turn to find Mark rushing toward me, his face a mask of tension.

"Everything okay?" I immediately ask.

"They say she's ready to push."

"That's good news," I assure him.

He doesn't look like he believes me. "I don't know who this woman is. I've never heard so much cursing in my life."

I have to bite my lip to keep from laughing. I remember this part too. Cassie had made me feel about an inch tall with her sharp tongue while she was delivering Kelty. She'd even smacked me because I was breathing too loudly.

"Hang in there, man. She'll be back to her old self once that baby is born."

"Fuck, I hope so. This Cassie scares the crap out of me. You've done this before, maybe you should go in."

This time I don't hold back and laugh out loud. "Fat chance of that, my friend. She's all yours. You'd better get in there before you miss the best part. We'll be in the waiting room, cheering you on from a distance."

"Asshole," he mumbles, but grabs onto me when I give him a quick hug.

"You'll be fine. Trust me on this."

He nods once, and walks back down the hall, his pace a little slower.

Entering the waiting room, I have to disappoint Kelty when I mention her mom's a little too busy right now for visitors. Mika's gentle reminder that she'll be a big sister soon puts a smile back on her face.

Forty-five minutes later, a rather disheveled looking, but broadly smiling Mark sticks his head around the door.

"It's a boy. Isaiah."

Mika

. . .

"I THINK AFTAH THIS WEEKEND, it's time for me to head back home."

I've just started counting the little holes in the ceiling tiles again, in an effort to pass time, when Jude's dad speaks up.

"Don't you like being with us, Grampa?"

He smiles at Kelty and I'm struck by the similarities I suddenly see between Jude and his father. "Oh, but I do, Peanut, and I'll still be comin' to visit, but I haven't seen mah friends in a good long while. Also been thinking about taking a trip on one 'a them cruise boats."

"Dad, you know we'd love for you to stay," Jude adds.

"I do, Son. I also know yaw stawtin' something new that don't need an old man hangin' around. Glad to see ya happy, though."

"Jim," I start, but he doesn't give me a chance.

"I was hawd on ya…regret that. Always wanted the best for mah boy, just took me a while to see maybe the best is just what yaw."

I grin at his gruff delivery, it's clear the man is marsh-mallow underneath. "Thank you, that's a really nice thing to say."

He harrumphs, brushing me off with a wave of his hand. "Time faw me to move out, and you to move in. Not like yaw not spendin' every night togethah anyways."

"You could've let me ask her, Dad," Jude says a tad irritated.

"Takin' forevah, Son. Didn't think you were evah gonna. Just movin' things along."

"Will you?" The question comes from Kelty and is directed at me.

I love that little cottage, but I would love waking up with

Jude, without him running off at the crack of dawn more. Besides, I've been thinking of another way to hang onto that cottage.

"I think if your dad would ask me, I'd probably say yes."

"Probably?"

I grin at an indignant Jude. "Yeah, it would depend on whether you'd be interested in letting me continue renting the cottage from you, so I could turn it into a photo studio and gallery."

"That'd be so cool," Kelty pipes up, her face all smiles as she looks expectantly at her dad.

"Sounds like I'm outvoted," he grumbles playfully.

"Bullocks," Jim says, and I start giggling just as the door opens and a grinning Mark sticks his head in.

———

So tiny.

I zoom in on Kelty's hand carefully cradling her brother's little foot as she counts his toes. He's perfect. The surprisingly thick, dark blond hair hides his slightly cone-shaped head and his face is pure perfection, with the same little button mouth Kelty still has.

"He looks like you, honey," I tell her, as I zoom out to capture Cassie gently pressing her lips to the little boy's head just as her daughter kisses his foot.

I've been snapping like crazy since Mark proudly introduced us to Isaiah. Pictures of Mom and Dad with baby, pictures of honorary grampa with baby, and a few with Jude holding that little bundle with Kelty looking on. Some great shots, but I already know this last one will be my favorite.

"Put that camera down for a minute, Mika," Mark says. "Don't you want to hold him for bit?"

I hesitate, looking at Cassie first, who just smiles at me. "Absolutely," I finally say, handing my camera to Jude.

Mark takes Isaiah from his wife and hands him to me. I immediately bring the tiny boy to my nose, closing my eyes as I inhale his baby scent deeply. When I peek up, Jude is looking at me with a deep concern in his eyes. I try to reassure him with a smile.

"We do have something to ask you, Mika," Mark announces, breaking through my thoughts as I see him share a significant look with his wife. She grabs his hand and entwines their fingers. "You should probably sit down first, though." He waits until I have a seat before he continues, "Cassie and I would like to name our son, Isaiah Jameson Sommers, if that's okay with you."

Immediately my eyes blur with tears and I can't even see Jude stepping closer, but I can sense him.

"We want to make sure he'll always be a part of this family," Cassie adds in a kind voice.

"Thank you," I choke out before burying my nose in the little baby bundle.

With Jude's hand on my neck grounding me, and Kelty's sweet weight leaning into my side, I feel my heart heal a fraction more.

Epilogue

Jude

"If you don't ask her, I will."

My eyes drift outside, where the first snow of the season is starting to come down.

"It's not that simple, Cassie."

"I know it's not, but the longer you wait the harder it'll be. It's in two days, Jude. Do you think she's not been aware of the date?"

"I'm sure Mika's well aware, but that doesn't make it any easier to tell her about—"

"Tell me about what?"

I look up to find the subject of our discussion standing in the doorway of my office, a scowl on her face.

"Busted," Cassie snickers in my ear. "I'll leave it in your capable hands."

"Thanks," I mumble, but I don't think she heard me; the line is already dead.

"Tell me about what?" Mika repeats sharply when I put down my phone.

"Baby, come sit," I plead.

"I think I'd rather stand for this, thanks."

I have to bite down a grin at her sharp sarcasm, because I have a feeling that wouldn't go over to well right now.

"All right. I'll tell you." I get up and walk toward her, noticing how she folds her arms over her chest when I get close. "That was Cassie, she's been on my case to talk to you about a party she's organizing for Kelty."

"So why haven't you?" she asks, looking at the ground but not before I see a flash of hurt in her eyes.

Fuck.

"Because she has it scheduled for this Saturday."

She lifts her face, a confused frown between her eyebrows. "Saturday?"

"The one-year anniversary of Jamie's death, I know, babe. But it's also been a year since Kelty's transplant."

"I know that, Jude. Why do you think I've been at the cottage all morning, baking her a cake?"

Shit. Don't I feel like an idiot? "I thought—"

I feel her hand on my chest. "I get what you thought, and I appreciate you trying to protect me, but you're missing the point here." She steps closer and loops her arms around my neck, looking up at me with those gorgeous blue eyes. "I've celebrated that heart beating for thirteen years. My son may be gone, but that heart is still beating, and I'll be damned if I stop celebrating it now."

"Fuck, baby." I tighten my arms around her until she is plastered against my front. "I love you so goddamn much."

"I love you too, but you'd better get on that phone and call Cassie back to tell her we've already got a cake, or I may reconsider."

Mika

To say I'm a little nervous is an understatement.

It's the middle of the day and the house looks packed. From what Cassie's told me over the phone yesterday, I'm about to meet both her family and Mark's.

I've gotten to know the Parks family pretty well, these past few months, so I know there'll be at least a few familiar faces.

I haven't been around a lot of people outside of the restaurant. Aside from a few visits to Boston, I've been focusing on my photography, editing the massive amount of images I took over the summer, and turning the cottage into a cute little gallery. I display my prints as well as the work of some local artisans. Trisha told me about her sister, who makes gorgeous jewelry from sea glass, and I'd been surprised to discover Giles has a knack for wood-working, and creates the most amazing sculptures out of driftwood.

I'm in my element there, and I can handle people if they don't know me from Adam, but a houseful of Kelty's family members—who all know who I am and what day this is—may be a bit much.

"Come on," Jude says, walking ahead up the driveway, carrying the cake I made. "It won't be nearly as bad as you think."

I'm not too sure about that.

It's Kelty who opens the door, a huge smile on her face.

"Can I see?" I guess her mom told her I'd be bringing cake.

"You can see later," Jude says firmly. "Hello would be nice just about now, though."

She grins up at him and plasters herself against him. "Hi, Daddy."

"Hey, Princess."

Then she turns to me, trying very hard not to stare at the big parcel I have in my hands as she gives me a hug. "Happy heart birthday, honey," I tell her, dropping a kiss on her head.

She leans back and looks up at me. "Are you sad?" She asks me that from time to time, and I try to be truthful.

"I'd be lying if I said no, but it's funny: today I'm sad and happy at the same time."

"Wanna feel?" She takes my free hand and presses it to her chest, where I feel her heartbeats steadily under my palm.

"I love you, honey." I smile down at her, and her bright blue eyes smile up at me.

"Love you too, Mika."

I'VE FORGOTTEN the names of half the people I was introduced to, but everyone's been really nice.

Still, I volunteered to change Isaiah so I could have a little breather. I'm upstairs in his gorgeous nursery when Jude walks in.

"You're timing is off, honey," I tell him, peeling back the tabs on the baby's diaper.

"Jesus," Jude blurts out, his hand slapping over his nose. "That can't be normal."

"You're such a lightweight. I bet you changed plenty of Kelty's diapers."

"Yeah, but I'm pretty sure hers didn't smell like that," he claims.

I grin and shake my head, quickly getting rid of the offensive diaper before cleaning Isaiah up and putting on a fresh one.

"That's better," Jude says, reaching around me to pick the baby up.

"Hey, that's not fair," I protest, but he just smiles and walks right out the door with him.

"Time for presents. Our princess is waiting."

Kelty is the center of attention when we get downstairs, and I'm suddenly a little self-conscious at the prospect of giving her my gift in front of a full house.

Jude is standing across the room next to his father, but when his eyes find me, he hands Isaiah off to Mark and makes his way here. When Kelty starts unwrapping presents, his arm is firmly around my shoulders.

"You may not know everyone, but I promise every soul here will feel the significance of your gift."

He saw it this morning. I'd just picked it up from the printer and unwrapped it to check, when he walked into the cottage. In hindsight I'm glad he did: it had been an emotional moment for both of us.

"Daddy, I'm opening yours," Kelty calls out.

"It's actually partly Mika's as well. You'll see."

She opens the box and pulls out the silver chain and beautiful intricately wrapped silver pendant, holding the red piece of sea glass I found. "It's so pretty. Can you put it on, Dad?'

Jude briefly lifts his arm from my shoulders and fastens the chain's clasp behind her neck. She turns to give him a hug, before giving me one too.

"Yours is next," she singsongs over her shoulder, walking up to the wrapped frame leaning against the wall.

It takes her all of two seconds to rip off the paper. When

she sees the print she looks at me with big eyes. "Is that him?"

"Yes, that's Jamie."

I'd promised her a picture of him, but it took me a while before I felt ready to share him.

I hope I'm ready now.

The print is a composition, the bottom a close up of Jamie's smiling face—a picture I snapped of him at a Red Sox game a few years ago—and the top is a recent shot I took of Kelty at the beach. The two images are joined by a red graph line.

"What's that red line?" Kelty asks, and I glance over at Cassie, seeing the transformation on her face when she realizes what it is. Immediately her eyes seek me out and her feet are already moving in my direction.

Her hug is tight, but so is mine.

Keeping her arm around my waist, she turns us to her daughter and I can feel Jude close behind me.

"That's your heartbeat," I explain. "It's the heartbeat that Jamie shared with you."

SUPERIMPOSED on the steady rhythm of their joint heartbeat are the words:

when hope ends…life begins

About the Author

Award-winning author Freya Barker loves writing about ordinary people with extraordinary stories. Driven to make her books about 'real' people; she creates characters who are perhaps less than perfect, each struggling to find their own slice of happy, but just as deserving of romance, thrills and chills in their lives.

Recipient of the ReadFREE.ly 2019 Best Book We've Read All Year Award for "Covering Ollie, the 2015 RomCon "Reader's Choice" Award for Best First Book, "Slim To None", and Finalist for the 2017 Kindle Book Award with "From Dust", Freya continues to add to her rapidly growing collection of published novels as she spins story after story with an endless supply of bruised and dented characters, vying for attention!

https://www.freyabarker.com

If you'd like to stay up to date on the latest news and upcoming new releases, sign up for my newsletter:
https://www.subscribepage.com/Freya_Newsletter

Also By Freya Barker

ARROW'S EDGE MC SERIES:

EDGE OF REASON

PASS SERIES:

HIT&RUN

ON CALL SERIES:

BURNING FOR AUTUMN

COVERING OLLIE

TRACKING TAHLULA

ROCK POINT SERIES:

KEEPING 6

CABIN 12

HWY 550

10-CODE

NORTHERN LIGHTS COLLECTION:

A CHANGE OF TIDE

A CHANGE OF VIEW

A CHANGE OF PACE

SNAPSHOT SERIES:

SHUTTER SPEED

FREEZE FRAME

IDEAL IMAGE

PORTLAND, ME, NOVELS:

FROM DUST

CRUEL WATER

THROUGH FIRE

STILL AIR

LuLLaY

(a Christmas novella)

CEDAR TREE SERIES:

SLIM TO NONE

HUNDRED TO ONE

AGAINST ME

CLEAN LINES

UPPER HAND

LIKE ARROWS

HEAD START

CPSIA information can be obtained
at www.ICGtesting.com
Printed in the USA
LVHW041037210320
650782LV00009BB/25

9 781988 733456